Torah To Telos:
The Passing of The Law of Moses

From Creation to Consummation

A multi-volume study of the passing of the Law of Moses

VOLUME #1

MATTHEW 5:17-18

"Not one jot or one tittle shall pass from the law until it is all fulfilled"

Unless otherwise noted, all scriptural citations are from the New King James Translations 1990, 1985, 1983, Thomas Nelson, Nashville, Tn.

ISBN 978-1-937501-05-1   1-937501-05-1

Produced by JaDon Management Inc.
1405 4th Ave. N. W. #109
Ardmore, Ok. 73401

Original Cover Design by:
Joseph Vincent
Contact Joseph at: joslau26@gmail.com, if you would like to consider using his services for your book or other creative designs.
Joseph resides in Kansas City, U.S.A.

Foreword

While all futurist eschatologies focus on the "end of the age" one of the most ignored, yet critical questions is "The end of what age?"

It is assumed by virtually all futurist schools that the end of the age is a referent to the end of time, the end of the Christian age.

I suggest that this "pre-assumption," is the cause of a theological tragedy of massive proportions. In fact, it is this very presupposition that continues to lead to wild speculation that "the end is near!" This misunderstanding demands the end of what the Bible affirms, repeatedly and emphatically, is without end– the Christian age.

Lying at the root of this eschatological confusion is the idea of the end of the Christian age. In fact, Biblically, the fulfillment of all prophecy, at the end of the age, is posited at the end of the Old Covenant age of Israel– at the end of Torah.

Over the last several years the issue of the end of Torah has begun to receive more and more attention. And it is high time!

The NT writers say, repeatedly, that their "one hope" their eschatological hope, was nothing but the hope of Israel, found in the Old Covenant promises made to Israel "after the flesh." You would think that this undeniable fact would cause advocates of a future coming of the Lord to reconsider their views that God was through with Israel and Torah at the cross, or even in AD 70. And thankfully, changes are taking place.

This book breaks new ground in the discussion of eschatology and its relationship to the passing of Torah. It is one of the most extensive examinations of Jesus' words in Matthew 5:17-18 to be found. With clear-cut logic and careful exegesis, the book presents a wealth of evidence to prove that Torah, the Law of Moses, did not pass away at the cross as commonly claimed, but, at the end of the Old Covenant age which occurred with the destruction of the Jerusalem temple in AD 70. This is when, according to our Lord's words, "All things written must be fulfilled" (Luke 21:22).

Table of Contents

3.) All just means the things dealing with Jesus' incarnation.

4.) All just means all things dealing with Jesus' death on the cross, where he fulfilled "all things"

5.) All just means the moral commandments, but not the cultic practices or the prophecies of the Old Law.

6.) All means that the Decalogue and Sabbath (but not the ceremonial law) remains valid until the "end of time." (Sabbatarianism).

7.) Related to points # 2 and 4– "All" really means that the prophetic element of the Old Law was not in fact "the law."

Page 151f – When Were All Things To Be Fulfilled?

Where does the Bible place the fulfillment of Torah? Is it at the end of the Christian age and time, or at the end of Israel's Old Covenant age? The answer is simple, but profound.

Page 170– A Response To Kenneth Gentry on Luke 21:22

Prominent Postmillennialist Kenneth Gentry claims to have found a major flaw in the preterist definition of "all things" in Luke 21:22. I respond to that article, demonstrating Gentry's major logical fallacies and false claims.

182f– A Summary of What We Have Seen

From Torah To Telos:[1]
The Passing of the Law of Moses

"Do not think that I am come to destroy the law and the prophets. I did not come to destroy, but to fulfill. For verily I say unto you, that until heaven and earth passes away, not one jot or one tittle shall pass from the law until it is all fulfilled" (Matthew 5:17-18).

To say the least, Matthew 5:17-18 is a text that perplexes many Bible students. Furthermore, to say that this text is the ground of many distinctive denominational doctrines is a huge understatement.

In this great verse Jesus sets forth the conditions for the removal of Torah, what we today call the Old Testament. That condition was the complete, total fulfillment / accomplishment of all that the Old Law looked forward to and predicted. Much more on this as we proceed in our study.

In Israel of Jesus' day, there was a somewhat divided view of whether the old Law would ever pass away. Some Jews believed that Torah was eternal, and would never pass away even when Messiah came and established the New Covenant.[2] Others believed that with the coming of the New Covenant, Torah would finally be removed.[3]

---

[1] The word *telos* is a Greek word, and often carries with it the meaning of both termination and *goal*. Thus, our title is suggestive that the end of the Old Covenant Law of Moses was likewise the goal of Torah. Paul said Christ is the end of the law for those who believe (Romans 10:4). With his coming, the beginning of the end of Torah began, and what is commonly called his second coming was the consummative *telos* – the goal of the previous ages (1 Corinthians 10:11).

[2] W. C. Allen, *International Critical Commentary, Matthew,* third edition, (Edinburgh, T and T Clark, 1957)45 gives numerous Jewish sources affirming the eternal nature of Torah.

[3] The writer of Hebrews is clear that the establishment of the New Covenant implied the removal of the Old (Hebrews 8:13).

Among many modern commentators Jesus' statement that "until heaven and earth passes away, not one jot or one tittle shall pass from the law" is taken to mean that Torah does indeed remain valid and binding until "the end of time." (Cf. Allen, op cit).

Among modern postmillennialists it is claimed that the law of Moses is eternal.[4] Gentry, commenting on Matthew 5:17-8, exemplifies the position of most postmillennialists today: "Christ has surpassed the legal foreshadows and rituals of the Old Testament." While maintaining that the cultic aspect of Torah has been removed, Gentry nonetheless posits the eternal nature of "the law of Moses.[5] He says that "heaven and earth" in Matthew 5:18 is the literal heaven and earth (*House*, p. 41).[6]

The late Greg Bahnsen, an outstanding apologist for the Theonomic movement, believed that "the law" will remain until the end of human history / the end of time. Let me summarize his comments on the Sabbath, which of course gives insight into his views of Torah.

---

[4]Actually, the postmillennial comments on Torah are mixed, to say the least. On the one hand Dominionists affirm the eternal validity of the Law of Moses, but then, they say that the Law of Moses passed away, either at the cross or in AD 70.

[5] Kenneth Gentry in *House Divided the Breakup of Dispensational Theology*, by Greg Bahnsen and Kenneth Gentry, (Tyler, Tx., Institute for Christian Economics, 1989)40. Gentry thus ignores Jesus' emphatic words that "not one jot or title shall pass from the law until it is all fulfilled." He wants to abrogate the ceremonial part of Torah, and keep the Decalogue, while ignoring the fact that the Sabbath is firmly embedded in the Decalogue! Thus, part of Torah could pass when part of it was fulfilled! As David Chilton pointed out in 1997, at a prophecy conference in Oklahoma City that I helped organize, the very verses that postmillennialists appeal to for support are actually their downfall! (Chilton's speech, along with the other presentations at that conference is available from me).

[6] Kenneth Gentry, *House Divided, The Break-up of Dispensational Theology*, (Tyler, Tx., Institute for Christian Economics, 1989)41.

1.) Sabbath is eternal and binding.

2.) Sabbath was part of the moral code: "Man's moral obligation to Sabbath observance is placed right along side the nine other universally moral words of the Decalogue, which was written by the very finger of God." (226).

3.) All men are subject to the Sabbath (226).

4.) "The Sabbath has universal extension and perpetual obligation." (226).

5.) "At the coming of Christ the Sabbath was *purged* of the legalistic accretions brought by the scribes and Pharisees (Luke 13:10-17; 14:1-6; Mark 3:1-6); the Sabbath had suffered corruption at the hands of the autonomous Pharisees just as numerous other moral precepts had (cf. Matthew 5:21-48). Moreover, the *ceremonial and sacrificial aspects* of the Older Testamental cycle of feast days ('new moon, Sabbath year, Jubilee, etc.) along with those cyclic observances of feast days, were 'put out of gear' by Christ's work of redemption. Hence, Colossians 2:16f loosens us from the ceremonial elements of the Sabbath system (the passage seems to be referring specifically to feast *offerings*), and passages such as Romans 15:5f and Galatians 4:10 teach that we need not distinguish these ceremonial days any longer (as the Judaizers were apt to require.)." (P. 226-227– all emphasis his)

6.) The Sabbath was a shadow of coming salvation under Torah– Sabbath is now a shadow of coming salvation. (227). "As Christ provides for entrance into eternal Sabbath rest of God by His substitutionary death upon the cross, He makes the typological elements (e.g. the offerings) of the Sabbath system irrelevant (things which were a shadow of the coming substance according to Colossians 2:157; Hebrews 10:1,8). By accomplishing our redemption Christ also binds us to the observance of that weekly Sabbath which prefigures our eternal Sabbath (cf. Hebrews 4)" (P. 227). So, Sabbath was abolished, but, Sabbath was instituted.

6.) Sabbath is now Sunday (227).[7]

As is easily seen, Bahnsen, like Gentry and virtually all modern interpreters of Matthew 5:17-18 dichotomized the law. He posits the passing of some of Torah, and yet, the abiding, eternal validity of some.

The problem with the view that Torah will stand valid until the (supposed) end of time is that virtually none of those who espouse this view are anywhere near consistent in what they are saying. Let me explain.

On the one hand we are told that Torah will remain until the "end of time." On the other hand we are told that portions– *major portions*!**– of Torah have been annulled. This is a huge problem that is being glossed over by all three major views of "the end times."**

On the one hand we are told that Torah will remain until the end of time. On the other hand, we are told, as just seen in Bahnsen and Gentry, that *parts of Torah* have been abrogated. In fact, McDurmon, commenting on Hebrews 8:13 says: "The New had in fact made the Old obsolete: 'And what is *becoming obsolete* and growing old is *ready to vanish away*' (Hebrews 8:13) But as he wrote, in his time, the Old was *becoming* obsolete and was *ready* to vanish away. It has not yet been completely wiped out, but was certainly in its dying moments. It died in AD 70, when the symbols and ceremonies of that Old System– the Temple and sacrifices– were completely destroyed by the Roman armies."[8] (All emphasis his).

---

[7] Greg Bahnsen, *Theonomy in Christian Ethics,* (Nacogdoches, Tx. 2002)226f.

[8] Joel McDurmon, *Jesus V Jerusalem* (Powder Springs, GA., American Vision 2011)47. McDurmon is the head of Research at American Vision and I had a formal public

So, Theonomists insist on the one hand that Torah will remain valid until the end of time, yet, they insist that the Law of Moses "died in AD 70." Needless to say, this is a huge problem.

Does this not violate Jesus' statements that "not one jot or one tittle shall pass from the law until it is all fulfilled"? How can it be argued that Torah – *any of Torah*– remains valid, yet some parts, indeed some *major, crucial elements*, have been nullified and removed. Do you see the problem?

How could Bahnsen affirm that: "Every single stroke of the law must be seen by the Christian as applicable to this very age between the advents of Christ."(Bahnsen, *Theonomy*, P. 81)– and yet argue that the sacrificial cultus is annulled, and is not, "applicable in this very age"? How can McDurmon say that the Law of Moses "died in AD 70" and then turn around and espouse the Dominionist theology, which is based on the (ostensibly dead) Law of Moses?

Bahnsen patently did not see his own inconsistency. Did Bahnsen believe that Christians are bound to the "strokes of the Law" that required circumcision? No. Did he believe and teach that Christians must make yearly pilgrimages to Jerusalem, as demanded by the multiple strokes of the Law (Exodus 34:24)? Did he teach that followers of Christ must offer up the bloody sacrifices demanded by the manifold "strokes of the Law"? No.

Furthermore, virtually all Theonomists appeal to the Old Law for a futurist eschatology. But again, how do you affirm that the Law of Moses died in AD 70 and then appeal to that dead law– with its festal calendar that typified the eschatological consummation– for your eschatology.

Gary DeMar, president of American Vision, says that all the cultic festivals were fulfilled:

"The New Testament describes Jesus as the fulfillment of every element of the Old Covenant shadows, feasts included (Passover, Unleavened Bread, Firstfruits, Pentecost). "And beginning with Moses and with all the prophets, (Jesus) explained to (His disciples) the things concerning Himself in all the Scriptures. . .. That all the things which are written about (Jesus) in the Law of Moses and the Prophets and the Psalms must be fulfilled"

---

debate with him in July 2012.

(24:27, 44). Earlier in Luke's Gospel we read "that all things which are written" about the end of the Old Covenant were "fulfilled" (21:22). Jesus is the "lamb of God" (John 1:29, 36), the temple (2:29), the bread from heaven (6:48), the high priest (Heb. 5:10), and the Rock (1 Cor. 10:4)."

He adds: "One of the first things a Christian must learn in interpreting the Bible is to pay attention to the time texts. Failing to recognize the proximity of a prophetic event will distort its intended meaning. The New Testament clearly states that the 'end of all things' was at hand for those who first read 1 Peter 4:7; that is, the Old Covenant with its types and shadows was about to pass away."[9]

DeMar also affirms that all of God's promises to Israel have been fulfilled:

"Non-dispensationalists like me would say that all the promises made to Israel have been fulfilled, and the redemption of Israel according to those promises made it possible for Gentiles to be grafted into an already existing Jewish assembly of believers that the Bible calls the Church. Soon after Jesus' ascension, the gospel is preached to "Jews living in Jerusalem, devout men, from every nation under heaven" (Acts 2:5)."[10]

It is patently illogical to claim that all of God's promises to Israel have been fulfilled, that all of the types and shadows of the Law have been fulfilled, and still hold to a futurist eschatology. DeMar has, like all postmillennialists and virtually all amillennialists, failed to see that all eschatological promises are posited at the end of Israel's age. They have failed to see that the types and shadows of Israel's feast days pointed directly to the eschaton. This is a glaring oversight in the Dominionist movement.[11]

---

[9] Gary DeMar, *Last Days Madness*, (Powder Springs, GA, 1994)27.

[10] http://americanvision.org/1728/all-promises-made-israel-have-been-fulfilled-answering-replacement-theology-critics-part-4/

[11] I should take note of a new brand of postmillennial eschatology that is springing up. Men such as James Jordan, Mike Bull, Ken Talbot, Peter Leithhart, Joel McDurmon, etc.

So, Bahnsen, Gentry, DeMar, McDurmon and the Theonomic movement, for all of their insistence that the Law of Moses is binding and eternal, are not the slightest bit consistent. David Chilton, a former Theonomist, noted this in a speech given in Oklahoma City, in 1997.[12]

---

are now affirming that all of Israel's promises were indeed fulfilled in AD 70 and that it is vital to see that event as redemptively significant. However, Gentry and most other postmillennialists are saying that, "God is preparing to punish His people Israel, remove the temple system, and re-orient redemptive history from one people and land to all peoples throughout the earth (Matthew 8:10-11; 21:43; John 4:23). This dramatic redemptive-historical event not only ends the old covenant era, but points to the end of history itself" (*Dominion*, 2009, 342). While affirming that AD 70 was the consummation of Israel's history- and eschatology- they say that the real story of eschatology is unrelated to Israel's eschaton, and is "Adamic Eschatology." This completely overlooks the (indisputable) fact that throughout scripture, both Old and New, the Spirit posits the fulfillment of Adamic Eschatology at the end of Torah, not at the end of human history as Gentry claims. In my debate with James Jordan, we covered this issue extensively, and Jordan was never able to counter it. That debate is now available in book form my websites, Amazon, and other retailers.

AD 70 did not point to a greater eschaton unrelated to Adamic eschatology. As a final note, it is ironic that for all of the epithets thrown at true preterists because preterism is not found in the creeds, *this new brand of postmillennialism is no where to be found in any of the creeds!*

[12] I personally helped organize that seminar. In his presentation, Chilton gave some of the reasons for his acceptance of the full preterist view, and exposed a few of the major fallacies of the Theonomic paradigm. He powerfully demonstrated that the very verse that Bahnsen and Theonomists appeal to for the enduring validity of the law (Matthew 5:17-18) actually falsifies that doctrine. Chilton's speech is available from me at my websites.

7

This is no minor theological issue. This is crucial for it reveals that the modern views of Torah and the doctrine of eschatology[13] are being radically misunderstood. Let me illustrate.

Gary North cited Deuteronomy 8 claiming that, "This passage in Deuteronomy presents the biblical basis of progress in history." He then added, "Any attempt to renounce this passage as no longer judicially binding in the New Covenant era is inescapably a denial of any biblical basis for God honoring cultural progress in history."[14]

What North– and those who follow him– fail to see is that Deuteronomy 8 mandates the obedience to *the Law of Moses*, which those same Theonomists insist "died in AD 70" (DeMar, McDurmon, et. al). How can you say that Deuteronomy 8 serves as the foundational, indispensable text for Theonomy, and then say that the Law of Moses died?

How can it be affirmed that the Law of Moses "died in AD 70" and then turn around and say that Deuteronomy 8– i.e. *the Law of Moses*– serves as the indispensable foundation for the modern Theonomy movement? That is saying that a dead law is the foundation of Dominionism!

North is espousing nothing short of a modified Judaizing movement. Of course, he would vehemently deny this, maintaining that he does not impose physical circumcision as the Judaizers of

---

[13] It is not just the doctrine of eschatology that is impacted by the views noted above. Ecclesiology, soteriology, and pnuematology are all directly impacted by the suggestion that part of Torah has passed while some remains valid. We clearly cannot develop all of these issues in this smaller work, however.

[14] Gary North, *Millennialism and Social Theory*, (Tyler, Tx., Institute For Chrisitan Economics, 1990)52f.

Acts 15 and the first century generation did. But this is what I mean by "modified." While he would not impose the sacrificial system of Israel, he assuredly is advocating the imposition of the Law of Moses onto the Gospel. He is putting new wine in old skins, new cloth onto old, contra Jesus' words in Mark 2:21f. His comment that Deuteronomy 8 is "judicially binding in the new covenant era" cannot be construed in any other way.

North is one of those who believes that when Jesus said "until heaven and earth passes, not one jot or one tittle shall pass from the law" that he referred to the literal cosmos. But of course, North likewise says that the sacrificial and ceremonial aspects of the Law of Moses has been annulled. It is therefore, incumbent on North and all of those positing the passing of *any aspect of the Law of Moses* to discuss the identity and definition of "the heaven and earth." To state the problem for all who say that some parts of the Law of Moses have passed, let me state it simply:

Jesus: Not one iota of Torah, (The Law of Moses) would pass until "heaven and earth" passed away.

"Heaven and earth" i.e. the literal, material universe, has not passed away.

Therefore, not one iota of Torah, (The Law of Moses) has passed away.

It simply will not do to say, *as the majority of commentators do*, that some of the Law has passed, but some remains. This is a direct contradiction of Jesus' words. He said none would pass until all was accomplished.

So, if one identifies and defines the "heaven and earth" of Matthew 5:18 as the physical heaven and earth,[15] then there is no way around it: Torah, *every jot and every tittle,* remains valid, binding and

---

[15] I might add that the same difficulty is found with Matthew 24:35. It is interesting that in the postmillennial literature, this verse is given little attention, except Jesus' affirmation that his word will never pass away. Little comment is offered as to the identity of the "heaven and earth" that would pass.

obligatory. Is there a proper, scriptural alternative to defining Jesus' use of the term "heaven and earth" as the visible, material cosmos? Yes, there is, but, we must step outside of our modern (Western) understanding of cosmology, language and literature to understand it.[16] I will address this topic below, but for now, let me explain what I mean by this by offering a word or two about proper hermeneutics and the application of cultural context.

---

[16] See my *Have Heaven and Earth Passed Away?*, or, my, *The Elements Shall Melt With Fervent Heat*, for a fuller discussion of how the ancient Hebrews used this term. Both books are available from Amazon, my websites, and other retailers.

SOME PRINCIPLES FOR BIBLE INTERPRETATION

It is sometimes difficult for modern readers to grasp the idea that Westerners think differently and read literature differently from how the ancient Hebrews did. How many times have we heard it said: The Bible says what it means and means what it says!"? I have had numerous people object, strenuously, to my insistence that we read the Bible through "Jewish" eyes, with an understanding of their culture, their world-view, their literature. I mean, after all, the Bible was written by "Jews" to Jews, about Jewish promises.[17] Does it not make sense to honor that context?

And yet, far too few Bible readers seem to be aware of how far modern students are from understanding the actual *sitz em leben* (the real life situation) of the ancient Hebrews. Perhaps even more disturbing, there are many who seem *unconcerned* with honoring that original context in the discussion of the modern interpretation of scripture. This is a major problem.

Wallace and Rusk discuss the disconnect between modern readers and the ancient context. They say that it is now well proven by "historical Jesus research" that there is, "a huge mismatch between early Christian doctrines and the post-Reformation doctrines."[18] They note that "several core doctrines that came from the Reformation have become the accepted tradition of many Christians today. These doctrines have become 'how its always been' and 'what everyone agrees on'. Christians often see them as 'the gospel' as Christianity itself. Many of us rely on them as comprising the safe, time tested majority view. They form part of our creed" (p. 7). However, they continue: "In light of recent scholarship, that very pursuit may oblige us to move away from some of their theological conclusions. Let us keep in mind, then, that although post-Reformation doctrines have become today's traditions, they carry little weight if they do not match the original Christian teachings" (*Transformation*, 2011, 9).

---

[17] It is better, probably, to say, by *Hebrews*, but, we use the term Jew due to its popularity.

[18] A. J. Wallace and R. D. Rusk, *Moral Transformation*, (New Zealand, Bridgehead Publishing, 2011)5.

What Wallace and Rusk are saying is that today, we know more about the true historical, cultural, social and theological world of the NT writers than we ever did, and that this better, more accurate knowledge of their world gives us a greater ability to properly interpret the scriptures.

In similar vein, McGuckin says, "There is a world of difference between the Semitic idioms of theology used in the ear of Jesus and his contemporaries and the Hellenistic modes of exegesis employed by the later fathers. The writings of the latter, though nearer the time of the biblical era, are not thereby guaranteed to have a deeper understanding of the Semitic idiom than that possessed by contemporary scholarship. Indeed, often the opposite is the case."[19] McGuckin is expressing something very profound.

Hays adds his comments: "The Christian tradition early on lost its vital connection with the Jewish interpretative matrix in which Paul had lived and moved; consequently, later, Christian interpreters missed some of Paul's basic concerns."[20]

And, here is the point in regard to Matthew 5:17-18.

Is it possible that Jesus and the NT writers and audience used the term "heaven and earth" idiomatically in ways that you and I are not familiar? Is it possible that in certain contexts, in certain settings, that this term was not intended to be a referent to the literal "heaven and earth", but to something that had nothing to do with sky and dirt? We shall see below that this is not only possible, but, probable.

The influence of the Hellenistic (Grecian) world view on the patristic writers is seldom given enough consideration by modern readers. And yet, thankfully, an increasing number of scholars and Bible students are realizing the critical importance of going back to the Jewish context of scripture to properly understand what they were saying, and how the original readers of what they said would have understood.

---

[19] John Anthony McGuckin, The *Transfiguration of Christ in Scripture and Tradition, Studies in the Bible and Early Christianity,* Vol. 9, (Lewiston/ Queenston, Edwin Mellen Press, 1986)Introduction.

[20] Richard Hays, *Conversion of the Imagination,: Paul as Interpreter of Israel's Scripture,* (Grand Rapids, Eerdmans, 2005)43.

Although they were speaking on the subject of marriage and divorce, Instone-Brewer's comments are ever bit as applicable to the subject at hand, the proper historical context for interpreting the Scriptures: "The early church was soon separated from the Synagogue and the Jewish world was itself cut off from part of its past by the destruction of Jerusalem. Background knowledge that could be taken for granted in the original readers of the New Testament disappeared from the Church. The misunderstanding that resulted, especially in the teaching on divorce and remarriage, have continued to the present."[21]

In comments that would have a direct bearing on our subject, Snyder says that Biblical eschatology is "radically disjunctive."

"It affirms the absolute validity of God's promises to mankind through Israel and of the historical locus of its fulfillment; yet denies that present history or the present institutions of man could lead to its fulfillment.".... "Paul proclaimed this eschatological form not only in terms of mythology of the cross, but also with a more full orbed apocalyptic framework. In the Hellenistic world this apocalyptic form was understandably misunderstood. In some instances it was literalized dualistically (i.e. the myth becomes a cosmology) so that a struggle between flesh and spirit resulted. In some instances it was misunderstood chronologically (i.e. the myth becomes history), so that an actual end of time was expected...the chronological misunderstanding resulted in a problem regarding the delay of the parousia to such a point that the community was forced to identify that disjuncture with the baptism or the birth of Jesus rather than to speak of a radical disjuncture yet at hand...in other words, the problem of the delay of the parousia is a problem only in so far as the early community misunderstood and literalized the apocalyptic."[22]

Snyder is clearly positing a heavy Hellenistic influence on the understanding of the "Jewish" scriptures, and this influence led to a belief in an "end of time" i.e. the end of literal "heaven and earth."

---

[21] David Instone-Brewer, *Divorce and Re-Marriage in the Bible*, (Grand Rapids, Eerdmans, 2002)Intro, p. X.

[22] Graydon Snyder, "The Literalization of the Apocalyptic Form in the New Testament Church," Chicago Society of Biblical Research, Vol. 15, (1969)5-18.

Although not discussing eschatology, Wallace and Rusk nonetheless discuss the heavy impact of Hellenism as a detriment for the proper understanding of scripture (*Transformation*, 2011, 16f).

Finally, Wilson summarizes the reality of the issues confronting the modern Western reader of the Bible: "The writers are Hebrew, the culture is Hebrew, the religion is Hebrew, the traditions are Hebrew, and the concepts are Hebrew."[23]

Why have we presented this kind of testimony? Well, if the Jews / Hebraic way of thinking, speaking and writing was different from the Grecian way of doing things, then it is distinctly (or at least) *possible* that when Jesus mentioned the passing of "heaven and earth" that he was using a Hebrew idiom that was never intended to be taken in a woodenly literal sense to indicate the end of the physical creation.

Am I suggesting that the Hebrews never used terms to speak of the literal, material "heaven and earth"? No. Am I suggesting that it would have been impossible for Jesus to predict such an event? No.

What I am suggesting however, is that before the modern reader automatically "jumps the gun" and assumes, without in-depth analysis of Hebraic terminology, Hebraic prophecy and Jewish thought, that Jesus had to be speaking of the ultimate end of material creation, it is in fact wise to at least consider that his referent to the passing of heaven and earth was a hyperbolic, metaphoric expression. And in point of fact, we need to insert this thought: those who claim that Jesus was referring to literal creation then turn around and claim that Torah has passed. So, here is what we have (and there will be more on this later):

Until "heaven and earth" passed, not a single iota of Torah would or could pass away (Jesus).

But, per all futurist views of eschatology, at least some of Torah, some of the jots and tittles, (e.g. the festal, sacrificial and ceremonial "jots and tittles) have in fact passed away.

Therefore, of necessity, "heaven and earth" have passed.

---

[23] Marvin Wilson, *Our Father Abraham*, (Grand Rapids, Eerdmans, 1989)29.

14

Jesus' words are clear and unmistakable, "until heaven and earth passes, not one jot or one tittle shall pass from the law." The passing of heaven and earth and the passing of the jots and tittles are synchronous events. Thus, to argue as all modern evangelicals do, that parts of Torah have been removed is to demand that "heaven and earth" have passed. *You cannot have the passing of Torah without the passing of heaven and earth.* It is therefore, the epitome of self contradiction to say that Torah has passed, but that "heaven and earth" have not passed, or that "heaven and earth" is referent to the literal cosmos.

Thus, the unanimous conviction of all futurist views that Torah has passed demands that we entertain the idea that Jesus was using the term "heaven and earth" in a metaphoric, figurative sense. Furthermore, as we will see below, the prophetic, theological and cultural context in which Jesus spoke lends support to the idea that he was using the term in a non-literal manner.

Amazingly, some claim that Jesus never used the term "heaven and earth" in non-literal ways. Thomas Ice, responding to some of my articles, claims that Jesus never used the term "heaven and earth" metaphorically.[24] But let's look at that for a moment.

Ice's contention that the term "heaven and earth" is not used metaphorically falls to the ground in Matthew 5.17f. As we have seen, Jesus said "until heaven and earth pass away, not one jot or one tittle shall pass from the Law, until it is all fulfilled."

The topic here is the Mosaic Covenant, Torah. Jesus said "heaven and earth" would not pass until the entirety of that Mosaic Torah was fulfilled. *Thomas Ice believes that the Mosaic Covenant, i.e. Torah has indeed passed away* (*Prophecy Watch*, 258). If therefore, the Mosaic Law has passed away, then the "heaven and earth" of Matthew 5 has passed away.

The dilemma here is acute for Dr. Ice. If he admits that the "heaven and earth" term is used metaphorically here, then his contention that the term is never so used falls to the ground. On the other hand, if he maintains his denial that the term is used metaphorically, then that

---

[24] Thomas Ice, "An Interpretation of Matthew 24-25" (part 32), http://www.pre-trib.org/article-view.php?id=233.

means that until literal "heaven and earth" passes away, Torah remains valid. This would demand that the Mosaic Law remains valid today. Ice cannot have it both ways.

> **You cannot, logically, argue on the one hand that "heaven and earth" in Matthew 5:18 refers to the literal cosmos, and then maintain that Torah has passed. Jesus is clear: Torah would only pass when "heaven and earth passed."**

In light of all of this, there is a legitimate question: Did the ancient Jews– including Jesus and the NT writers– expect the end of the physical cosmos?

Needless to say, there are scholars who believe that the references to the passing of "heaven and earth" are indeed predictions– failed of course– of the end of time, or the destruction of physical creation. Dale Allison (private correspondence) has expressed this, and Adams recently (2007) produced a monograph in which he responds to N. T. Wright, France and others who say that the Jews did not have a doctrine or concept of "the end of time."[25]

On the other hand, Mayor claims that *the dominant view* of ancient Rabbis was that the world / creation is permanent and will never pass away. He cites Ps. 148:4-6 and 104:5 as corroborative.[26] Wright affirms that when the NT writers spoke of the impending, "end of the age"

---

[25] Edward Adams, *The Stars Will Fall From the Heaven,* (New York, T and T Clark International, 2007). I personally find Adam's tome unconvincing. He ignores the fact that many of the OT prophecies of the destruction of "heaven and earth" are said by later writers to have been fulfilled (e.g. Psalms 18 describes David's deliverance from Saul in terms of cosmological dissolution; Malachi 1:2 with referent to Isaiah 34. Isaiah 64 records the prayer for YHVH to come out of heaven as he had come in the past).

[26] Joseph Mayor, *The Epistle of St. Jude and the Second Epistle of St. Peter,* (Eugene, Or., Wipf and Stock Publishers, 1907/ 2004)162, n. 2.

that: "The close of the age for which they longed was not the end of the space order, but the end of the present evil age."[27] R. T. France says, "The unwary reader is in danger of assuming a note of finality in the future hope of the Old Testament that is in fact foreign to it. The "eschatology" of the Old Testament prophets was not concerned with the end of the world, but with the decisive act of God which will bring to an end the existing order of things in the world, and inaugurate a new era of blessing, of a totally different order."[28] France also stated: "Where Jesus used the symbolic language of the Old Testament, it is perverse to look for a literal application of his words." (France, 1982, 236).[29]

Brown, commenting on the language of Christ's coming in Matthew 24:29f, concurs that this language is from the OT and that there is no justification for taking it literally. It is metaphoric language to describe Jehovah's powerful intervention into history, not to end history."[30]

Milton Terry, author of the highly respected works on *Biblical Hermeneutics* and *Biblical Apocalyptics*, commented on the metaphoric use of "end of the world" language employed by the OT

---

[27] N. T. Wright, *Jesus and the Victory of God*, (Minneapolis, Fortress Press, 1996)341; 345-346; 361-362.

[28] R. T. France, *Jesus and the Old Testament*, (Grand Rapids, Baker, 1982)84.

[29] France's asservation raises a serious hermeneutical issue. If it is perverse to literalize the symbolic language of the OT when the NT writers utilize that language, it eliminates any possibility of a future "end of the world." All NT eschatological predictions are based on and taken directly from that OT metaphorical pool of language. Every NT writer emphatically tells that their expectation of the eschaton was what was promised in Torah. Thus, to admit, as France, Wright and a host of other scholars do, that it is wrong to take that OT language literally, even when the NT writers use it, is a powerful demonstration that the NT writers were not, in any text, anticipating the end of time.

[30] Colin Brown, *New International Dictionary of New Testament Theology*, vol. 2, (Grand Rapids, Regency Reference Library, Zondervan, 1986)35f.

17

prophets, and said: "When the leading OT prophets makes use of such language in foretelling the desolation of Edom, with what reason or propriety can we insist on the literal import of such passages as Matthew 24:29 and 2 Peter 3:10?"[31]

He later adds: "When we come to study the doctrines of biblical eschatology, how little do we find that is not set forth in figure or in symbol? Perhaps the notable confusion of modern teaching on the subjects of the parousia, resurrection and judgment is largely due to the notion that these doctrines must needs have been revealed in literal form" (Terry, *Hermeneutics*, 594).

So, it is clear that there is a scholarly acknowledgment that the language of the passing of heaven and earth should be understood metaphorically, and not literally. It is misguided to posit a woodenly literal interpretive matrix on top of the Biblical text and ignore the Hebraic forms of expression that tended (properly understood) more toward figurative expression than literalism. With this in mind, let's turn to an examination of how the Biblical prophets utilized the language of heaven and earth. We will examine the prophetic background of the term heaven and earth, and then turn to an examination of how the Jews in the first century used the term.

---

[31] Milton Terry, *Biblical Hermeneutics*, (Grand Rapids, Baker,)446.

HAVE HEAVEN AND EARTH PASSED AWAY?

Some years ago I wrote a book entitled, *Have Heaven and Earth Passed Away?*[32] In that book I established that throughout the OT the prophets anticipated and predicted imminent various "Days of the Lord" in which YHVH described His actions within history as if history was coming to an end. The fact that these OT prophets used such graphic "de-creation language" is inescapably true, unless a person is married to a woodenly literalistic hermeneutic that insists on ignoring the metaphoric nature of Hebraic thought and literature.

Sadly many Bible students are unfamiliar with the apocalyptic and figurative language of the Bible. So many people like to say, "The Bible says what it means and means what it says." They seem to be saying there is no such thing as figurative or spiritual language. This is sad because a *lot* of the Bible is symbolic language. The term heaven and earth is a good example. (We are not saying the term heaven and earth never refers to material creation. We are saying this term is very often used figuratively).[33]

Let me give here a few examples, taken from my book, in which the OT prophets foretold the destruction of "heaven and earth."

In Isaiah 13, Jehovah foretold the destruction of the grand city Babylon (v. 1). The prophecy was fulfilled initially within 15 years when the Assyrians sacked and pillaged the city. Interestingly, even some leading dispensationalists are forced to acknowledge the metaphoric nature of Isaiah's language.

Walvoord and Zuck commented on Isaiah 13: "In Isaiah's day that judgment was coming because of the tremendous political turmoil of the next several decades that would culminate with the fall of Babylon at the hands of the Assyrians in 689 BC. .... the statements about the heavenly bodies no longer functioning may figuratively describe the total turnaround of the political structure of the Near East. The same would be true of the heavens trembling and the earth shaking, v. 13,

---

[32] Available on my websites, Amazon, and other retailers.

[33] In my *The Elements Shall Melt With Fervent Heat*, I show that it was the "heaven and earth" of Israel that was the focus of prophecy, not material creation.

19

figures of speech suggesting all-encompassing destruction." (P. 1060)–
"The word 'them' against whom the Medes were stirred up (v. 17)
were the Assyrians referred to in v. 14-16, not the Babylonians. It
seems better to understand this section as dealing with events
pertaining to the Assyrian's sack of Babylon in December 689 BC."[34]

This is quite a remarkable admission from leading dispensationalists.

Note that in verse 10-13 Isaiah said that in that destruction, "The
stars of heaven and their constellations shall not give their lights. The
sun will be darkened in its going forth, and the moon will not cause its
light to shine…Therefore, I will shake the heavens and the earth will
move out of its place in the wrath of the Lord of Hosts." What was
happening is Isaiah used hyperbolic, metaphoric language to describe
the fall of Babylon. The *world* of the Babylonians came crashing down
around their ears. Their "heaven and earth" was destroyed, because
their capital city, the center of their world, fell. I think it is pretty clear
that literal, physical heaven and earth was not destroyed when Babylon
fell, right?

Another example is Isaiah 34. The language is graphic. It describes
the dissolution of "heaven and earth" along with all the constellations.
However, it is a prediction of the fall of the Edomite kingdom. Years
later, Jeremiah (Jeremiah 25), and Ezekiel (Ezekiel 35) and the book
of Obadiah reiterated the prediction of Edom's fall, using the same
language. It *sounded* like the destruction of "heaven and earth," and
was, but it was not the end of physical creation. It was the end of the
world of Edom. Edom fell to the Babylonians in BC 583 just a few
short years after the Chaldeans had destroyed Jerusalem in BC 586.
The book of Malachi actually looks back on the destruction of Edom
as a historical fact (Malachi 1:2).

So, in each of these cases, and there are many others, "heaven and
earth" was destroyed. But again, it is clear that the "heaven and earth"
in view was the world, the society and the culture of the kingdom that
was destroyed. Their world was destroyed, so, their heaven and earth
was destroyed. And, the Old Testament predicted that the time was
coming when Israel's "heaven and earth" would perish as well.

---

[34] John Walvoord and Roy Zuck, *Bible Knowledge
Commentary* Vol. I, (Wheaton, Ill, Victor Books, 1985)1059f.

As we suggested above, the problem with most modern day readers of prophecy and scripture is that we most commonly approach the Bible as if it were a modern book, written in the modern vernacular of people raised in a Grecian world view and vocabulary. But nothing could be further from the truth.

The Bible is full of Hebraic idiom, euphemism, etc. and is thoroughly Hebraic in all ways. Let me give again McGuckin's quote from above: "There is a world of difference between the Semitic idioms of theology used in the ear of Jesus and his contemporaries and the Hellenistic modes of exegesis employed by the later fathers. The writings of the latter, though nearer the time of the biblical era, are not thereby guaranteed to have a deeper understanding of the Semitic idiom than that possessed by contemporary scholarship. Indeed, often the opposite is the case."[35]

As Beale wisely suggests: "The Bible was written in very specific circumstances and the better one understands these surrounding circumstances the more rich one's understanding of the Bible may become."[36] Holland also makes a very pertinent point: "While the vocabulary of the NT could be found throughout the Hellenistic world, it did not have the same meaning when it was used in the religious sense within the Jewish community."[37]. Holland notes that when a NT writer wrote in Greek it was. "Hebrew in its mind-set and essential meaning." (P. 52).

What I am suggesting is that Jesus' use of the term "heaven and earth" was a Hebrew idiom of the day, and not a woodenly literalistic cosmological statement. I am suggesting that modern Bible readers are, as implied by Beale, sadly out of touch with the "surrounding

---

[35] John Anthony McGuckin, *The Transfiguration of Christ in Scripture and Tradition, Studies in the Bible and Early Christianity*, Vol. 9, (Lewiston/ Queenston, Edwin Mellen Press, 1986)Introduction.

[36] G. K. Beale, *The Temple and the Church's Mission*, (Downer's Grove, Ill., InterVarsity, 2004)31.

[37] Tom Holland, *Contours of Pauline Theology*, Christian Focus Publications, Geanies House, Fearn, Ross-Shire IV20 1TW, Scotland, UK, 2004)252.

circumstances" of the Biblical narrative, and as a result we tend to define and interpret scripture from a skewed perspective.

Another OT prophecy of the passing of "heaven and earth" will substantiate what I am saying. For a complete discussion of the issue see my *The Elements Shall Melt With Fervent Heat.*[38]

The prophet Isaiah predicted the passing of heaven and earth in chapter 24.[39] He said the earth would be "utterly broken down, clean dissolved and completely removed" (v. 19). This sounds like the destruction of material creation, but closer examination reveals it to be speaking of the destruction of Israel's Covenant World under the imagery of "heaven and earth."

Note that verse 5 gives the reason for the destruction, "they have broken the everlasting covenant." What covenant was that? It was *the Mosaic Covenant*! The Mosaic Covenant was the "everlasting covenant" of "the city of confusion," i.e. Jerusalem, mentioned in verse 10.

McDurmon takes note that Isaiah's referent to "the earth" should more properly be "the land" and "the passage clearly applies to a people who broke the everlasting covenant, and these could only be Israel at that time."[40]

---

[38] Available from Amazon, my websites, and other retailers.

[39] The many direct parallels between Isaiah 24-27 and Revelation 20-22 are significant. It should be patently obvious that Revelation was anticipating the consummation foretold in Isaiah (including of course chapters 64-66). The incredible thing is, of course, that as noted, Isaiah was predicting the arrival of the new, resurrection world, as the climax of Israel's covenant history. There is nothing even remotely resembling an "end of time" or the end of human history" in Isaiah. It is therefore wrong to project that concept into Revelation, since John is clear that he was looking for the fulfillment of what the OT prophets foretold (10:6-7).

[40] Joel McDurmon, *Jesus V Jerusalem, A Commentary on Luke 9:51-20:26: Jesus' Lawsuit Against Jerusalem,* (Powder Springs, GA., American Vision, 2011)59.

Of course, what McDurmon fails to see, or to acknowledge, is that this destruction, the ensuing New Zion, the establishment of the rule of YHVH on Zion, is the time when, "He shall destroy death" (25:8). In other words, the eschatology of Isaiah 24-25 is the source of Paul's resurrection doctrine in 1 Corinthians 15, the end of the millennium resurrection. For McDurmon to acknowledge, therefore, that Isaiah 24-25 speaks of the "the clearly covenantal judgment" on Israel is a tacit admission that the resurrection of the dead occurred in AD 70, at the end of her Covenant "heaven and earth." The resurrection of Isaiah 24-25 is inseparable from that "clearly covenantal judgment."

So, God would destroy "heaven and earth*" because Israel had broken her covenant with Jehovah*. Will the universe be destroyed because Israel will break the *Mosaic Covenant*? Wouldn't that demand that at some point the Mosaic Law would have to be restored?

I am unaware of *any* school of interpretation that teaches that one day God will destroy the literal creation because of Israel's violation of *the Mosaic Covenant*. But, Isaiah 24 speaks of the destruction of "heaven and earth" because of Israel's violation of the Mosaic Covenant. It is clear therefore, that the "heaven and earth" that God would destroy because of Israel's rebellion had to be a metaphoric "heaven and earth."

A dilemma is created for the literal interpretation of the text when we come to verse 22. In these verses God is depicted as dwelling gloriously in Mount Zion, that is, in Jerusalem, *after the destruction of heaven and earth*.[41]

If the earth has been destroyed how could literal Mount Zion still exist? The best explanation is to see that Isaiah was predicting the destruction of Israel's *covenant* heaven and earth because she had violated the Mosaic Covenant with Jehovah. As a result God's

---

[41] Isaiah 65-66 likewise foretold the destruction of the old heaven and earth, and the coming of the New Creation at the time of the judgment of Old Covenant Israel. See my lengthy discussion of these texts in my *The Elements Shall Melt With Fervent Heat.*

righteousness would remain in a New Zion--in a new *covenant* heaven and earth. He was going to create a New Zion.[42]

A look at one final OT prophecy of the passing of "heaven and earth" is in order, since the prophecy is cited in Hebrews 1, and is a favorite "text of appeal" for those affirming the passing of literal "heaven and earth."

Psalms 102:25-28:

> "Of old You laid the foundation of the earth,
> And the heavens are the work of Your hands.
> They will perish, but You will endure;
> Yes, they will all grow old like a garment;
> Like a cloak You will change them,
> And they will be changed.
> But You are the same,
> And Your years will have no end.
> The children of Your servants will continue,
> And their descendants will be established before You."

As is so common when a passage is appealed to for proof of a given doctrine, no consideration is given to the actual context of the text. Words that sound like they teach a given, presuppositional doctrine are found, and made to fit. The reality is that Psalms 102 just does not predict the end of the literal "heavens and earth."

Space will not allow a full development of the text, but note the other Messianic elements found in this great chapter. These other constituent elements are inseparable from the prediction of the passing of the heaven and the earth.

➡ V. 12-16– The redemption of Zion; "You will have mercy on Zion"; "The Lord shall build up Zion."

➡ v. 16– The appearing of the Lord in glory.

➡ v. 18- The creation of a New People.

---

[42] In both the OT and the New, there is a doctrine of the Two Jerusalems. The Old Covenant, earthly Jerusalem and the New, Heavenly Jerusalem. In a multitude of OT prophecies, we find on the one hand the utter desolation of one Zion, but, in the same context, we find the exaltation of Jerusalem, and the description of the glorified Zion does not fit any description of the earthly. See my *Who Is This Babylon* for an extended discussion of this highly important doctrine.

➡ v. 20 - The deliverance of the prisoners.

➡ v. 20 - The resurrection, i.e. the releasing of those "appointed for death."

➡ v. 22 - The gathering of the people to the Lord.

➡ v. 28 - The abiding of the seed of the Lord.

Now, anyone remotely familiar with these Messianic motifs, and the New Testament application of these tenets, will realize immediately that none of these elements can be harmonized with the idea of "the end of time." It simply will not work. Let me illustrate.

➡ V. 12-16– The redemption of Zion; "You will have mercy on Zion"; "The Lord shall build up Zion."

In Messianic prophecy, Zion is the locus of the Day of the Lord (Isaiah 59). It is where the Messianic Banquet is established at the time of the resurrection of the dead (Isaiah 25:6-8). It is the fountain from whence the New Covenant flows (Isaiah 2:2f). It is the place where salvation is posited (Isaiah 46:13). To put it in short form, Zion is the capital of the eschatological kingdom.[43]

While a great deal could be said about Zion, we will forego this discussion to just below.

➡ v. 16– The appearing of the Lord in glory

Note that the Psalm likewise foretold the appearing of the Lord in glory. The New Testament writers are very clear in their expectation of that coming in glory. It was at hand in the first century (Matthew 24:30f; 25:31f; 26:64). Thus, the motif of the coming of the Lord in glory is one that is posited by scripture as destined for fulfillment in the first century. This logically demands that no matter how we might perceive the nature of the destruction of "heaven and earth" that since that destruction and the coming of the Lord in glory are connected, that the NT writers were likewise anticipating the passing of "heaven and

---

[43] William Bell and I co-host an Internet radio program entitled Two Guys and the Bible, at AD 70.net. We engaged in an extensive discussion over several weeks, of the issue of Zion. Those programs are archived for listening at www.AD70.net.

earth" in their generation. On this note, see Jesus' words in Luke 21:25-32.

➡ v. 18- The creation of a New People

The Psalmist predicted the creation of a New People. This is where it gets especially problematic for all futurist eschatologies.

There are no futurist eschatologies that posit the creation of a new people, thus a new covenant people, at the end of the Christian age, or the end of time. Yet, the Psalmist is clearly anticipating such an event in his words about a "people to be created."

What many people fail to note is the perfect correspondence between Psalms 102 and Isaiah 65 (and 66).

In both texts we have the destruction of creation (Isaiah 65:17f). We have the creation of New Zion (65:19). We have the creation of a new people (65:15f).

What stands out in Isaiah is that this new creation would arrive when Israel had filled the measure of her sin (v. 6f) and YHVH destroyed her (v. 13f). It is that destruction that would lead to the new creation / new people.[44]

Now, unless one could exegetically demonstrate that the Psalmist had a different time, a different eschaton in mind from that of Isaiah, then unless all three futurist views are willing to now create a doctrine of the creation of a new people at the end of time, then we must honor the context of Isaiah 65-66. And that means that the new people to be created when the "heavens and earth" would pass away– no matter how we define them– would be the new covenant people of Messiah.

That means that Psalms 102 cannot be referent to some proposed end of time, or the end of the Christian age. The New Covenant people were fully formed when the Old Covenant people was destroyed, for filling the measure of their sin (cf. Matthew 23; 1 Thessalonians 2:14-16; Revelation 6:9f)– in AD 70.

---

[44] Paul's use of Isaiah 65 is significant. He quotes directly from Isaiah 65:1-2 in his discussion of Israel's recalcitrance and the resultant calling of the Gentiles via his ministry in Romans 10:20f. For Paul then, the time of the eschaton had arrived and was present in his ministry.

➡ v. 20 - The deliverance of the prisoners

The parallels between Psalms 102 and Isaiah continue in this motif. In Isaiah 61 the prophet looked for the coming of Messiah to proclaim the "acceptable Day of the Lord." Of course, Jesus cited this verse as he stood in the synagogue of Nazareth, and declared, "Today this scripture is fulfilled in your hearing" (Luke 4:21).

So, Psalms 102 foretold the time when the "prisoners" would be given freedom. Isaiah reiterates that prophecy, and Jesus applies that prophecy to his ministry and his message. This can only mean that the time for the passing of "heaven and earth" had arrived in the first century. There is no huge temporal gap between Jesus' message of liberty and the someday, sometime, one of these days, passing of the old creation.

The liberty promised to the captives would be found in the redeemed Zion of Psalms and Isaiah 61. Be sure to read our comments just below about this much anticipated salvation in Zion. Simply stated, Hebrews affirms in unequivocal language that the promised time of the redemption of Zion had arrived: "You have come to Mt. Zion!" The importance of this cannot be over emphasized.

➡ v. 20 - The resurrection, i.e. the releasing of those "appointed for death."

An in-depth discussion of this would take us too far afield. Suffice it to say that we find here the resurrection motif. Those "appointed for death" were none other than the "prisoners." We are dealing here with a Hebrew parallelism. The reason for this that in the ancient times, to be in prison was, for all practical purposes, to be doomed to death. To be in prison was to be "dead."

Of course, if there is a connection between the prisoners and those "appointed for death" and of course the connection is clear, then when Jesus declared that the time for the fulfillment of Isaiah 61 had arrived, he was likewise saying that the time for the fulfillment of Psalms 102 had arrived.[45]

---

[45] See my *Seventy Weeks Are Determined...For the Resurrection*, for an in-depth discussion of the resurrection and its first century fulfillment. The book is available on my websites, from Amazon and other retailers.

➡ v. 22 - The gathering of the people to the Lord

The gathering of the people to YHVH is a dominant Messianic and eschatological theme.[46] It is found extensively in Isaiah, Jeremiah, Hosea and other of the prophetic books. What should not be missed is that, just like the resurrection, just like redemption, just like the creation of the New People, the locus of that re-gathering is invariably posited in "Zion."

Notice in Isaiah 11:10 we find the prophecy of the setting up of the "banner" or ensign, to which the gathering of the people would flow. This is the Second Exodus, when the dispersed of Israel would return to the Lord: "He shall set up an ensign for the nations, and shall assemble the outcasts of Israel, and gather together (*sunesei*) the dispersed of Judah from the four corners of the earth" (v. 12).

In Romans 15:12f, Paul cites Isaiah's prophecy and applies it to his day, and the calling of the nations to Christ. Clearly, the gathering of the people had begun. And, since Genesis 49:10 posited the gathering of the people to "Shiloh"[47] in "the last days" we have clear cut testimony to the time of the fulfillment of Psalms 102.[48]

Isaiah 62 likewise foretold the setting up of the ensign or banner for the gathering of the people:

"Go through, Go through the gates! Prepare the way for the people; Build up, Build up the highway! Take out the stones, Lift up a banner for the peoples! Indeed the Lord has proclaimed To the end of the world: "Say to the daughter of Zion, 'Surely your salvation

---

[46] See my *We Shall Meet Him In The Air, the Wedding of the King of kings* or a fuller discussion of this very important theme. That book is available from my websites, Amazon, and other retailers.

[47] Shiloh, in Genesis 49 seems to mean "peace maker" or something like that. We are reminded of Ephesians 2:15f "he is our peace"!

[48] Needless to say, that if the gathering of the people of Isaiah 11 was taking place in Paul's ministry then the dispensational doctrine of the postponement of Israel's kingdom is falsified. Paul clearly was citing Isaiah as being fulfilled in his day and in his ministry. He knew nothing of a postponed kingdom.

28

is coming; Behold, His reward is with Him, And His work before Him. And they shall call them The Holy People, The Redeemed of the Lord; And you shall be called Sought Out, A City Not Forsaken."

Notice once again that just as the passing of the heavens and earth in Psalms 102 is tied, three times, to the redemption of "Zion" Isaiah also posits the "gathering" to the banner, at the time when Zion would be "established" (*diorthosis*, v. 7),[49] the city no longer called forsaken. This is the time of salvation.

Of course, it would be remiss of us to fail to note that this coming of the Lord for the salvation of Zion is cited by Jesus in Matthew 16:27-28 and fulfillment emphatically placed in Jesus' generation.

It should be more than evident from the above that Zion is the central focus, the locale if you will, of the eschatological hope of Psalms 102 and a host of other prophecies. In other words, Psalms 102 foretold the gathering of the people to Messiah, the creation of a new people, the time of the resurrection and the removal of "heaven and earth." And all of this is posited in "Zion."

With this in mind, it is important to see that in Hebrews 12:18f, the inspired writer affirms that the Old Covenant "heaven and earth" delivered at Sinai was on the verge of being removed. Also, he said his audience had come to "Zion," and that they were in the process of receiving the kingdom that can never be moved (12:26-28).[50]

---

[49] The use of *diorthosis* here is highly significant. It is used to speak of the "restoration" of Zion. In Hebrews 9:10 the author uses diorthosis to speak of the consummation of Israel's prophetic hopes, expressed in the festal cultus of the temple. That cultus was prophetic of "the time of reformation" (diorthosis). See my extended discussion of the correlation between the diorthosis, the time of reformation, and the eschatological consummation of the restoration of all things (*apokatastasis*) of Acts 3:21-24. That discussion is found in my Like Father Like Son, On Clouds of Glory book, available from my websites, Amazon, and other retailers.

[50] Throughout scripture, the New Jerusalem and the New Creation is invariably posited at the time of the dissolution of Old Covenant Israel. It is never at the end of the Christian age. This is the glaring, inescapable, insurmountable

A significant number of scholars recognize that Hebrews 12 is not discussing the passing of literal creation.[51] Lane argues, with excellent analysis, that Hebrews is discussing the passing of the Old Covenant World.[52] Among postmillennialists, it is a virtual "given" that Hebrews 12 was fulfilled in AD 70 with the removal of the Old Covenant world of Torah.

In discussing the "role call of faith" in Hebrews 11, Keith Mathison says, "Under the New Covenant we *have come* to Mt. Zion. We *have come* to the heavenly Jerusalem. We *have come* to the church of the firstborn. We *have come* to Jesus, the mediator of this glorious New Covenant.... That which the Old Testament believers looked for in faith has come, and they have now received what was promised"[53]

Likewise, Joel McDurmon, with whom I had a formal public debate in July, 2012, says that the faithful of Hebrews 11 have received the kingdom.[54] Gentry adds:

---

problem in all futurist eschatologies. See my *The Elements Shall Melt With Fervent Heat*, for a full discussion and demonstration of this.

[51] The direct parallels between Isaiah 24-25 and Hebrews 11-12 should be noted carefully, but we will not do that here.

[52] William Lane, *Word Biblical Commentary*, Hebrews, Vol 47b, (Dallas, Word, 1991)480.

[53] Keith Mathison, *Postmillennialism, An Eschatology of Hope*, (New Jersey, P & R Publishing, 1999)135. His emphasis.

[54] McDurmon conveniently omits the fact that the hope of all of those OT worthies was the heavenly city and country, and the *"better resurrection."* This is hugely problematic for McDurmon, Jordan, Talbot, Gentry, et. al. and other Dominionists who claim that Israel's eschaton was fulfilled in AD 70 but, that Edenic Eschatology remains unfulfilled until the end of the Christian age. Hebrews 11 clearly embraces the eschatological hope that extends all the way back to creation! Thus, to affirm, as these men do, that Hebrews 11-12 was fulfilled in AD 70, is a falsification of their eschatology. The indisputable fact is that all Biblical

"The writer of Hebrews contrasts the old covenant and the new covenant (Hebrews 12:18-28), pointing out that the new covenant recipients are currently receiving (*paralambanontes*, pres. act. prtcp) 'a kingdom which cannot be shaken' (Hebrews 12:28). This kingdom will 'remain' after God shakes down the old covenant order at the temple's destruction in AD 70. (Heb. 12:26-27; cp. 8:13), destroying those temple implements made with hands (9:11, 24; Mk 14:58; Acts 7:48). In Hebrews 1:3 we learn that 'when he had by himself purged our sins' He then 'sat down at the right hand of the Majesty on High' anticipating becoming his footstool (Heb. 10:13). The kingdom, which he receives in history, is unshakable and will 'remain' until the last enemy is vanquished (cp. Mt. 16:18)." (*Dominion*, 2009, 259).

It seems not to have dawned on Mathison, McDurmon, Gentry, and the Dominionists that if the promises of Hebrews 11-12 have become a reality and the Old Covenant faithful, "have now received what was promised," that this *demands* that *the resurrection has occurred.*

How the Old Covenant saints could have already, "received what was promised" and yet, are still awaiting what was promised, Mathison and the other Dominionist do not explain. They simply assert it. This is a contradiction of terms.

McDurmon has this problem, perhaps even worse. Like Mathison, Gentry, DeMar, etc. he says that the faithful of Hebrews 11 were given what they longed for.[55] But, like those other men, McDurmon is even more specific.

---

eschatology is incorporated into Israel's eschatology, to be fulfilled at the climax of her age.

[55] Interestingly, in his comments on Hebrews 11-12 and Luke 13:26f, McDurmon conveniently uses the word "kingdom" to speak of what Abraham and the worthies received. This diverts attention from the fact that what they were promised was *the New Creation* and the *"better resurrection."* To use these terms however, inextricably links what the worthies received with the eschatological consummation of 2 Peter 3, Revelation 20f, etc. and McDurmon cannot allow that connection and maintain his futurism.

Commenting on Luke 13:27f, McDurmon says that Abraham, Isaac and Jacob, all the OT worthies, entered the kingdom and sat down at the table, when the sons of the kingdom were cast out. Now, make no mistake: it is virtually universally recognized that the, "sitting down in the kingdom" of Luke 13 (parallel Matthew 8:11) is referent to the resurrection Banquet of Isaiah 25:6-8.[56]

Hagner says the language of Matthew 8, "Is to the eschatological banquet, a great time of rejoicing and feasting in celebration of the victory of God, anticipated in both the OT and NT (see Isaiah 25:6; Matthew 22:1-14; 25:10; Rev. 19:9; Luke 14:15-16."[57] France says of the language of the sitting down in the kingdom, "The imagery is that of the Messianic Banquet (cf. Matt. 26:29; Luke 14:15; 22:30), a prominent theme in Jewish eschatological expectation, derived from Isaiah 25:6."[58] Davies and Allison say, "In Matthew 8:11 and parallels the resurrection and the messianic banquet are in view. The redeemed will mingle with the fathers of Abraham at the great heavenly banquet."[59]

Finally, Filson says, "When the final Kingdom comes and the great Messianic Banquet occurs, many Gentiles will come from east and west and share in the banquet (cf. Isaiah 49:12 which, refers to the return of the scattered Israel, and 49:19) with the patriarchs of Israel, Abraham, and Isaac and Jacob (who in 22:32 indicates, will share in the resurrection). The sons of the kingdom, the jews, who by ancestry

---

[56] Commenting on Matthew 8:11 and Abraham sitting down in the kingdom, Nolland (NIGTC, Matthew, Grand Rapids, Paternoster, 2005)357, n. 44, says: "The imagery is taken from Isaiah 25:6."

[57] Donald Hagner, *Word Biblical Commentary, Matthew*, Vol. 33a, (Dallas, Word, 1993)205.

[58] R. T. France, *Matthew, Tyndale Commentary*, (Leicester, England, Intervarsity Press, 1987)156f.

[59] W. D. Davies and D. C. Allison, *International Critical Commentary, Matthew 8-11*, (London, T and T Clark, 2004)30.

would naturally be expected to share in the final kingdom, will be rejected."[60]

This kind of quote could be multiplied many times over. There is virtually no disagreement in the commentaries. Abraham and the faithful sitting down in the kingdom is a reference to Isaiah 25:6 and the end of the millennium resurrection.

So, with this in mind, let me make just a few observations that are relevant to our discussion.

Abraham longed for the heavenly country and city. He longed for the better resurrection (Hebrews 11:35). This is *critical*. Let me offer my thoughts as succinctly as possible.

The resurrection that Abraham longed for is the resurrection of Isaiah 25, *the end of the millennium resurrection of 1 Corinthians 15 and Revelation 20.*[61]

The resurrection of Isaiah 25 is at the time of the Messianic Kingdom (Wedding[62]) Banquet (Isaiah 25:6) established in "Zion" when Abraham and the worthies would sit down in the kingdom of Matthew 8. Here is what this means.

---

[60] Floyd Filson, *The Gospel According to Matthew,* (London, Adam and Charles Black, 1971)111.

[61] Paul explicitly says his resurrection doctrine would be in fulfillment of Isaiah 25 (I Corinthians 15:54f). Thus, unless one can demonstrate exegetically that Abraham was longing for a different resurrection from that promised in Corinthians / Isaiah, then the connection is firm.

[62] We cannot develop it extensively here, but, there is a direct link between Isaiah and the story of Hosea. In Hosea, God was married to Israel, but, she became a harlot wife, so, He *Divorced* her. When He divorced her, He *Departed* (5:15) from her, and she "*Died*" (5:14; 6:5). The story of redemption is the opposite side of that tragedy. YHVH promised to *Remarry* Israel (2:18-19) and when He did, He would *Return* to her *(5:15; 6:3)* and *Raise* her from the "dead" (6:2-3; 13:14). See my 30 lesson MP3 series on Hosea for a fuller discussion of these critical issues. The resurrection of Isaiah 25 is the resurrection of Hosea, and the Banquet of Isaiah 25 is the promised Wedding of Hosea. My series on Hosea is available from my websites.

☛ The Messianic Banquet of Isaiah 25:6 is at the end of the millennium resurrection of Isaiah 25:8. This is indisputably true since Paul says that the resurrection of 1 Corinthians 15 (which of course is the resurrection of Revelation 20:11-12) would be when Isaiah 25:8 was fulfilled.

☛ The Messianic (Resurrection) Banquet of Isaiah 25:6 is the fulfillment of the resurrection hope of Abraham, Isaac, Jacob, and all the OT worthies– all the way back to Creation (Hebrews 11:35).

☛ The Messianic (Resurrection) Banquet would be when Abraham, Isaac, Jacob and the OT worthies sat down in the kingdom (Matthew 8:11).

And what does McDurmon say about Matthew 8:11 (par. Luke 13:26f) and Abraham sitting down at that Messianic Banquet? He says that occurred in AD 70 in the casting out of the "sons of the kingdom" (2011, 64). McDurmon is not alone in this application of Matthew 8.

Many, if not most, modern postmillennialists likewise apply Matthew 8:11 to the end of Israel's covenant age in AD 70.[63] They patently do not see that this demands that the end of the millennium resurrection was in AD 70.

So, what we have from these postmillennial commentators is their conviction that the end of Torah and Israel was in fact in AD 70 (not the cross). But more, they are tacitly, but definitely inadvertently, positing the fulfillment of the end of the millennium resurrection as well.

By affirming that the OT saints received all that they were promised demands the fulfillment of their eschatological hope. In fact, in unguarded moments, postmillennialists affirm that very thing.

DeMar, writing in opposition to the dispensationalists, says, "All promises made to Israel have been fulfilled."[64] Likewise, Mathison, commenting on the prophetic hope of the faithful in Hebrews 11-12

---

[63] This is the view of Gentry (*Dominion* 2009, 342); DeMar (1994, *Madness*, 164), Mathison, (*Age*, 2009, 407+) etc.

[64] Gary DeMar, Internet Article, "Answering the Replacement Theology Critics" (Part 4), at: http://americanvision.org/1728/all-promises-made-israel-have-been-fulfilled-answering-replacement-theology-critics-part-4/.

says, "Christians are now experiencing the fulfillment of the eschatological hopes of Israel" (*Age*, 2009, 625).

Well, let it be clearly noted that if all of God's promises to Israel have been fulfilled, and if Christians today are "experiencing the fulfillment of the eschatological hopes of Israel" then it is indisputably true that the end of the millennium resurrection has occurred.[65] This is inescapable. The argument can be easily expressed like this:

All of God's eschatological promises to Israel have been fulfilled (DeMar / Mathison).

But, the end of the millennium resurrection was an eschatological promise made to Old Covenant Israel "after the flesh" (Romans 9:3).

Therefore, God's OT eschatological promise to Israel, of the end of the millennium resurrection, has been fulfilled and Christians are now experiencing the fulfillment of that promise.

There is simply no way to logically and consistently affirm, as these good men have, that God has fulfilled all of Israel's Old Testament promises, without affirming the fulfillment of the end of the millennium resurrection.

---

[65] The resurrection of 1 Corinthians 15 and Revelation 20, therefore, were the "eschatological promises" of Israel. In fact, Paul considered that resurrection as the *sine qua non*, the *epitome,* of God's eschatological promises of Israel's eschatological hope.

Postmillennialists, and amillennialists, stoutly affirm that God has fulfilled all Old Covenant promises to Israel.

They then affirm that God was through with Israel either at the Cross or in AD 70.

They completely overlook (or ignore) the fact that the end of the millennium resurrection was an Old Covenant promise, made to Old Covenant Israel, "after the flesh" (Romans 9:3).

It is therefore, the epitome of inconsistency to affirm that God fulfilled all OT promises to Israel, and then to affirm a yet future end of the millennium resurrection!

Notice the united eschatological narrative in Hebrews. The hope of all the worthies extends all the way back to Creation, i.e. Abel. This is one story, one hope, one eschatology, consummated when Abraham and the worthies would sit down at the Messianic Banquet table in the kingdom– in Zion. And the Hebrews author is clear: "you have come to Mt. Zion" (Hebrews 12:21).[66]

Here is the entire panoramic story of eschatology incorporated into the story of Israel, *fulfilled at Zion,* to which they had arrived. This is *Torah until Telos.* This is eschatological consummation at the end of Torah, not the end of the Christian age, not at the end of human history.

To say, as McDurmon and the postmillennialists do, that the worthies received the kingdom in AD 70 is just another way of saying that they

---

[66] The entire story of eschatology and soteriology is focused in and on "Zion." This is a hugely important topic. It is my intention to write a short work on this theme. It is impossible to over-emphasize the eschatological significance of the Hebrews authors' statement, "You have come to Mt. Zion."

were about to receive the heavenly country, the heavenly Zion, and *the end of the millennium resurrection.*

The problem for the postmillennialists and virtually all futurists is that they divorce Hebrews 11-12 from Revelation 20-22. On the one hand they tell is that the OT saints have indeed received the kingdom. They received what they were promised. But then, these same authors tell us that those saints are still awaiting the consummation of Revelation 20.

Did not those worthies long for the heavenly city (Zion, the New Jerusalem) and the heavenly country? Indeed, and that is precisely what Revelation 20-22 predicted. Did Revelation promise a different New Creation from that which all of the worthies, all the way back to creation longed for? Is the Zion of Revelation different from the eschatological hope of Abraham in Hebrews? Where is the slightest suggestion of this?

Do the OT saints "almost" have what was promised? Have they *partially* entered into the promised heavenly city and country? Have they received part of the "better resurrection"? Well, "Have received what was promised," is not the same as, "we await the consummation."[67] And affirming that Christians are "now experiencing the fulfillment of Israel's eschatological promises" is not the same as saying those promises are unfulfilled.

Thus, just as Isaiah foretold that Old Covenant Israel's heaven and earth would be destroyed and that God would dwell in Zion, Hebrews depicts the removal of the "heaven and earth" of Old Covenant Israel and God dwelling in New Covenant Zion forever (Hebrews 12:21-28). Patently, for the writer of Hebrews, the removal of "heaven and earth" did not involve the dissolution of material creation. It involved the passing of the Old Covenant World of Israel.

This reality is important for the futurist paradigms all of which claim that the Mosaic Covenant world ended at the cross, or even in AD 70.

---

[67] To be sure, there is an "already-but-not-yet" eschatology in the New Testament, as almost all scholars agree. However, what Mathison, et. al, fail to honor is that in the NT, the "not yet" i.e. the consummation to which Mathison refers, is *never* posited as far off. It is invariably at hand and coming soon. This is clear in the Hebrew declaration that those first century saints had arrived at Zion.

Even some who claim to be preterist have fallen (back) into the unfortunate position that, "National, ethnic Israel and the law of Moses were left behind at Calvary, and spiritual Israel and the gospel of Christ began."[68]

The fact is that in Hebrews 12 the writer affirms, unequivocally, that the "heaven and earth" of the Old Covenant world of Israel had not yet passed away, but, was on the verge of doing so. Furthermore, we must remember the text before us. Jesus said that until heaven and earth passed, Torah could not pass.

So, what we have seen is that the Jews and scripture used the term "heaven and earth" metaphorically to speak of the temple, the veil of the temple that contained the "elements" (*stoichiea*) of the world (*cosmos*). Even the priests' garments represented the heaven and earth.

The modern reader would be well served to consider this highly metaphoric, symbolic world of thought and expression when reading and interpreting the New Testament scriptures and the predictions of the destruction of "heaven and earth." There is no sound reason for assuming and presuming that when Jesus said "until heaven and earth passes, not one jot or one tittle shall pass from the law" that he had the material creation in mind.

---

[68] Kurt Simmons, April, 2011 "Sword and Plow" email journal. See my refutation of this unfortunate claim on my websites: http://www.eschatology.org/all-articles-articles-211/37-respon ding-to-the-critics/913-kurt-simmons-and-the-abandonment-of- biblical-eschatology. Kurt has become increasingly desperate and illogical in his attempts to deny the validity of Covenant Eschatology. Simmons is (now purposefully) ignoring the undeniable reality that the resurrection– which he posits as AD 70– was the hope of OT Israel. In our written debate, I asked him– many times– to explain how he could believe that Israel's hope (the resurrection) would not be fulfilled until AD 70, and yet claim that Israel and Torah, which promised her salvation / resurrection, was left behind at the cross? He never offered a word of explanation. Our formal written debate on the passing of Torah (*The Passing of Torah: At the Cross or AD 70?*) is available on my websites, on Amazon, and through other retailers.

And let me drive this home by reiterating something: All futurist eschatologies insist that Torah, the Law of Moses, did pass in the first century. So, Jesus said, "until heaven and earth passes away, not one jot or one tittle of the Law shall pass." Yet, all futurists say that the "jots and tittles" of Torah have passed. This logically demands that "the heaven and earth" that Jesus had in mind in Matthew 5 has indeed passed away. If one insists on maintaining that Jesus was referring to the literal creation, then one must abandon the view that Torah, any of it, passed away. There is no other choice.

The only solution to this conundrum is to admit that Jesus was using the term "heaven and earth" metaphorically as was common in the Hebraic world of his time.

If the "heaven and earth" that had to pass for Torah to pass was the literal, physical creation, then one must abandon the view that Torah– any of it-- has passed away. There is no other choice. After all, it is pretty clear that the physical cosmos has not passed away, isn't it?

THE PASSING OF TORAH AND ESCHATOLOGY

What many Bible students do not seem to understand is the critical relationship between the passing of Torah and eschatology, the doctrine the coming of the Lord, judgment and the resurrection. Let me explain.

As we have seen, all futurist views of eschatology claim that Torah, at least part of it, was removed at the cross, or perhaps in AD 70.[69] Furthermore, all futurist views of the coming of the Lord posit that event at the end of the Christian age.

However, when one looks closer, it is quickly discovered that there is a huge discrepancy in those same futurist views. At least two of those paradigms, (postmillennial and dispensational) while affirming that the Law of Moses has been abrogated, then turn around and appeal to the Old Testament for their eschatological hope.

Let me present here what all three of the futurist views (with some variations) believe about the Law of Moses. We will then turn our attention to the relationship between the fulfillment of Israel's promises and eschatology.

#1 – The Moral Law, i.e. the Ten Commandments, Remains Endlessly.

Postmillennial re-constructionists appeal to Matthew 5 to justify the imposition of the Law of Moses today.[70]

---

[69] In several formal written and public debates with amillennialists my opponents have all affirmed, some stridently, that God was through with Israel and Torah at the cross. In a 2011 written debate, my opponent Jerry McDonald affirmed that God had no relationship with Israel after the cross, and that the entirety of Torah, (with the exception of the prophecies of the last days events, of course) was removed at the cross. As we shall see, this dichotomization of Torah is unjustified. My debate with McDonald, and other of my written debates on the topic can be found on my websites: www.eschatology.org or www.bibleprophecy.com.

[70] Mathison, (Dispensationalism, 87-94) and virtually all Dominionists affirm "The Mosaic Law is (i.e. still today, DKP) God's Law." Yet, at the same time, they affirm that the Law of Moses was removed at the cross. What they really

Sabbatarians appeal to Matthew 5:17-18 to support their contention of the abiding nature of the Sabbath. Since "heaven and earth" are clearly still with us, they say, then Sabbath observance is still binding.

Of course, non-Sabbatarians dichotomize the Pentateuch, and even the Decalogue, and say that the Sabbath mandate, which of course sits squarely in the middle of the Ten Commandments, has been abrogated. They reject the Sabbatarian doctrine saying that it is "Judaistic" but then insist on the (typological) "Christian Sabbath" which finds no support whatsoever in Scripture. So, once again, some jots and some tittles of the Law have been abrogated, while some remains.

#2 – The "Sacrificial, Ceremonial law" Passed at the Cross.

All three futurist views insist that the ceremonial aspects of Torah, that is, the, "new moons, feast days and Sabbaths" (Colossians 2) were all removed at the cross.[71] Well, perhaps this needs some clarification.

All three futurist views say that the *sacrificial elements of Torah* were nullified. The amillennial and postmillennial writers are unanimously agreed that the entire ceremonial cultus was removed. However, the millennialists take a different tact.

Dispensational writers all agree that the "ceremonial law" was removed in Christ. By that they mean the sacrifices of Torah were fulfilled.[72] However, and this is *important*, millennialists then insist

---

mean is that "some jots and some tittles of the Law" were removed at the cross while *some* jots and tittles remain valid today.

[71] But of course, this is where one of the fundamental problems with millennialism appears. On the one hand they tell us that Colossians 2 speaks of the removal of the Law of Moses by Christ. On the other hand they tell us that the new moons, feast days and Sabbaths have yet to be fulfilled at the rapture, judgment and resurrection! Furthermore, they then tell us that these festal events will once again be mandated in the millennium, and failure to honor them will result in condemnation.

[72] There is a great deal self contradiction about this actually. Thomas Ice says that the true full meaning of the Old Covenant sacrifices will not be realized until the re-institution

that the final three of Israel's feast days, Rosh Ha Shanah (Judgment), the Second Coming (the consummation of the Atonement) and the feast of Harvest (the resurrection) must yet be fulfilled.

What the millennialists are conveniently and necessarily overlooking or ignoring is that those final three feast days were inextricably tied to the first four sacrificial Passover-Pentecost feast days. It was all one festal calendar.

Of course, all three futurist views insist that the Judgment, Second Coming and Resurrection have not yet happened. They fail to see that by positing those events in the future they are of necessity re-instituting Torah. The feast days constituted an integral part of the "jots and tittles" of the Law, did they not? And they were patently sacrificial in their very form and substance, were they not? They were ceremonial as well.

So, positing the eschatological consummation in the future, all the while saying that the "ceremonial and sacrificial" elements of Torah have been removed is inherently self contradictory. You cannot on the one hand say that the ceremonial and sacrificial element of Torah has been removed, and then say that you are looking for the future fulfillment of the ceremonial and sacrificial element of Torah.

---

of the temple cultus in the millennium: "The sacrifices of the millennium will not be a return to the Mosaic Law, since the Law has forever been fulfilled and discontinued through Christ (Romans 6:1, 15; 7:1-6; 1 Corinthians 9:20,21; 2 Corinthians 3:7-11; Galatians 4:1-7; 5:18; Hebrews 8:13; 10:1-14)." However, just a few pages earlier he wrote: "In the millennial temple, all that was prescribed and initiated in the Old Testament ceremonial and ritual activities will come to completion and their fullest meaning." Thomas Ice, *Prophecy Watch,* (Eugene, Ore, Harvest House, 1998)256, 258. So, on the one hand the law (which of necessity included the sacrifices) has been fulfilled in Christ, but on the other hand, those cultic sacrifices will not find their true fulfillment until the millennium!

You cannot affirm – as all futurist eschatologies do– the passing of all of the ceremonial and sacrificial elements of Torah i.e. the New Moons, feast days and Sabbaths, without thereby affirming that the judgment, Atonement and the resurrection promises were either nullified or fulfilled!

Those ceremonial, sacrificial mandates were inextricably part of "the law." Jesus said that not one jot or one tittle would pass from "the law" until it was all fulfilled.

So, if the cultic "jots and tittles" have passed, then the full preterist view of *Torah To Telos* is fully established.

#3 – Prophecies in the Old Testament Remain Valid and Will Only Be Fulfilled at the End of Human History.

Dispensationalists especially rely most heavily on the OT for their eschatology, believing that the OT promises were to and for Israel, while the New Testament promises and prophecies relate exclusively to the church.[73] Thomas Ice for instance, claims that Deuteronomy contains the prophetic "roadmap" for Israel's (still future) destiny.[74]

Postmillennialists and some amillennialists (e.g. Hoekema) appeal to the Old Testament for their belief in a future conversion of Israel at the end of the Christian age.

There is a sub-set of #3 held by a handful of preterists, and that is that the ceremonial laws were abrogated at the cross, while the eschatological promises of the OT remained valid until AD 70. The

---

[73] Ironically, even some postmillennialists affirm the same thing, as I will demonstrate below from Lorraine Boettner.

[74] Thomas Ice and Kenneth Gentry written debate: *The Great Tribulation Past or Future,* (Grand Rapids, Kregel, 1999)75–76.

43

Decalogue (with the exception of the *ceremonial, prophetic* Sabbath mandate, of course) remains valid today.

Kurt Simmons says: "Indeed, while the Old Testament was done away, most of the law *still exists* and condemns men of sin just as much as it ever did. If we will take the time to analyze it, we will find that the only law removed by the passing of the Old Testament was the ceremonial law and various incidental laws associated with Israel's nationhood, and that these had *nothing* to do with either condemning or justifying man."[75] One would be hard pressed to find a more self-contradictory and false statement or theology. Wasn't there a *death penalty* for violating or failing to observe the *ceremonial, prophetic, Sabbath* day?

The first thing that strikes one as they look at these tenets above is that they radically re-define Jesus', "not one jot or one tittle shall pass from the Law until it is all fulfilled." Note Simmons' "most of the law still exists...the only parts removed" claim. He– and those holding to a similar view– have *some* of the jots and *some* of the tittles passing, while *some* jots and *some* tittles remain valid!

The problem is that this redefines Jesus' reference to "all" the law being fulfilled and makes him out to say: "When *some* portion of *some* of the Law has been fulfilled, then *some* of Torah will pass." Isn't there something very badly wrong with any theology that has to turn Jesus' words on their head and in essence deny them?

All three futurist views say *"some* jots and *some* tittles of the Law have been removed, but *some* jots and *some* tittles remain." This turns Jesus' words on their head!

---

[75] Preston - Simmons Debate, Simmons' Second Affirmative, (Ardmore, Ok. JaDon Management Inc., 2010). Available at: www.eschatology.org.

It needs to be clearly understood that the distinctions that some try to make in "the law" are simply theological inventions that find no agreement in scripture or Jewish thought. Here is what I mean.

In both scripture and Jewish thought, while we find references to "the law, psalms and prophets" (Cf. Luke 24:44) even this breakdown gives no support for the threefold breakdown of "the law" delineated just above. There is no justification for a radical dichotomization of the law into moral code, ceremonial aspects and prophetic aspects that allows for some of Torah to pass while some would remain valid. As we shall see in the chapter "What Was 'The Law?'" below, the Jews knew nothing whatsoever of a definition of "the law" that excluded the prophetic books or the Wisdom books as "the Law."

We need now to address the topic of this chapter heading, and that is the relationship between the fulfillment of Israel's Old Covenant promises and prophecies, and eschatology.

ISRAEL, TORAH AND ESCHATOLOGY

As a young man growing up in the amillennial world, I heard countless sermons proclaiming the "truth" that God was through with Israel at the cross. When Jesus died on the cross, he nailed the "handwriting of ordinances" to the cross, removing Torah forever. It was almost a mantra cited countless times that Israel is no longer God's covenant people, and that beginning at the cross, or, perhaps as late as Pentecost, the Lord has been dealing with the church, the New Covenant people of Christ.[76]

In later years, in formal public debates, I have asked my amillennial opponents: "At what point of time, and in what events, were ALL of God's Old Covenant promises made to Old Covenant Israel fulfilled, and His Covenant relationship with them terminated?" Almost without

---

[76] There is tremendous controversy in the amillennial circles of my youth as to what covenant was in effect for the 50 days between the cross (where Torah was ostensibly removed) and Pentecost, when the New Covenant was "probated." I well remember lengthy, sometimes lively, discussions at seminar open forums, among preacher discussion groups etc.

fail, they have answered, "At the cross."[77] The point is that in amillennial circles Israel and the Old Testament plays virtually no role in eschatology. In the more scholarly amillennial circles there is tremendous ambiguity even today concerning Israel.

In regard to Israel and the fulfillment of her Old Covenant promises, Riddlebarger says: "Christ has fulfilled the Old Testament promises regarding the coming of the messianic age. The prospect of a future kingdom indicates that Christ's fulfillment of these Old Testament promises is typological of a more glorious and final kingdom yet to come" (2003, 113). He views the Old Testament promises fulfilled and a new set of promises given: "Because of Jesus Christ and his coming, the Christian possesses the complete fulfillment and blessings of all the promises of the messianic age made under the old covenant. But, the arrival of the messianic age also brought with it a new series of promises to be fulfilled at the end of the age. The fulfilled promises pointed to a more glorious and future fulfillment. This is called the 'not yet' or future eschatology. It is this already/not yet tension which serves as the basis for understanding much of the New Testament eschatological expectation" (2003, 61).

In a similar vein, Butler says, "There are no predictions of the Second Advent of the Messiah in the OT."[78] One can but ponder how Butler would seek to sustain such a claim when every single NT writer that addresses the parousia of Christ to any extent appeals directly to the OT promises of that event.[79]

---

[77] Something revealing has taken place, however. Some of my amillennial opponents in later debates were very familiar with the difficulties that earlier amillennial opponents encountered by giving the "orthodox view." So, they would rather evasively respond: "My hope is based on the entire Bible." However, when pressed, they would then admit that they believed that Torah passed away at the cross.

[78] Paul Butler, *Approaching the New Millennium: An Amillennial Look at AD 2000*, (Joplin, College Press, 1998)286+.

[79] As I have noted, I was personally raised in the theological paradigm espoused by Butler, and affirmed precisely what he says. It was a stunning, and unsettling,

So, on the one hand, God has fulfilled all of the Old Covenant promises to Israel. Christians have received all that was promised to Israel in the Messianic kingdom. But, due to the fulfillment of the Old Testament promises, "the messianic age brought with it a new series of promises to be fulfilled at the end of the age."

What is at work here is a subtle transition from "Jewish eschatology" to "Christian eschatology," what can also be called historical eschatology, i.e. the end of history.[80] There is, however, no doctrine of "Christian eschatology" to be found in the Old Covenant *or the New.*

Riddlebarger, representative of much of amillennialism, affirms the fulfillment of Israel's kingdom promises and the end of her age in the first century. But, the fulfillment of Israel's eschatological promises gave way to, and created a brand new, previously unknown / unrevealed "new series of promises to be fulfilled at the end of the Christian age." And in fact, per Butler, the Old Testament never even predicted the consummative eschaton. No matter how one might seek to disguise this, it is nothing short of "replacement eschatology."

In effect, Riddlebarger and amillennialism as a whole is guilty of a later version of what was happening in Romans 11. There, Gentiles claimed that God was through with Israel, and therefore, all promises now belonged to the church / Gentiles as opposed to Israel.

If God had already brought His dealings with Israel to a close, then of necessity, this demanded and demands that a "Christian eschatology" i.e. the end of the Christian age must be created. And this is precisely what is communicated by Riddlebarger's insistence that a "new series of promises" was delivered to the church, for fulfillment at the end of the Christian age.

Unfortunately for the amillennial paradigm, Paul emphatically denies that God was through with Israel *when he wrote.* That consummation would be at the coming of the Lord in judgment / salvation of Israel, in fulfillment of Isaiah 27 and 59.

---

discovery on my part to realize that all NT eschatology is derived directly from God's Old Covenant promises made to Israel "after the flesh" (Romans 9:3).

[80]See my MP3 series "All Israel Shall Be Saved," for a discussion of Romans 11:25f. The series is available from my websites.

The postmillennialists often express the same sentiments as the amillennialists in regard to Israel and eschatology. Boettner, a noted postmillennialist, said: "For information concerning the first coming of Christ, we go to the Old Testament. He came exactly as predicted and all those prophecies were fulfilled or were forfeited through disobedience. But for information concerning his Second Coming and what future developments will be, we go only to the New Testament."[81]

Likewise, while he does not express himself in the same emphatic manner, McDurmon's view is, *of necessity*, the same. As we have seen, he says the Law of Moses "died in AD 70." What this logically demands of course, is that if Torah died in AD 70, then Butler was right to say that the OT never predicted the final coming of the Lord. But of course, this is patently false.

If the NT is our exclusive source of information concerning eschatology and the Law of Moses died in AD 70, then it is patently wrong for any futurist to appeal to any OT prophecy given to Israel concerning the last days and Christ's parousia as unfulfilled. But of course, all futurists do appeal to the OT for prophecies of the end of the Christian age.[82]

The inherent contradiction here is more than apparent. On the one hand we are told that all of the OT promises to Israel are fulfilled– fulfilled no later than AD 70. On the other hand, we are told that OT promises made to Israel have not been fulfilled, and will not be fulfilled until the end of the Christian age (which supposedly has

---

[81] Lorraine Boettner, *Four Views of the Millennium,* (Downers Grove, InterVarsity, 1977)102.

[82] As we will demonstrate below, historically, Romans 11:25f has been a foundational text for the postmillennial futurist eschatology. It has been part of the Reformed creedal statements that Paul anticipated the conversion of Israel at the end of the Christian age. There is, however, a *radical* change taking place within the Reformed camp in regard to Romans 11. It is now not uncommon for Theonomists to acknowledge that Romans 11 was fulfilled in AD 70. This is the view of Jordan, DeMar, McDurmon and others. To say that this is a major paradigm shift is to massively understate the case.

nothing to do with the fulfillment of God's Old Covenant promises to Israel).

We could develop this issue much, much more, but the reader can readily see the problem. What we want to do now, ever so briefly, is to document the indisputable link between Torah and *Telos*, i.e. the relationship between the Law of Moses and the coming of the Lord, judgment and resurrection. To do this, I will lift some (revised) material from my book, *We Shall Meet Him In The Air, The Wedding of the King of kings*.

SACRED ? SPACE

☞ The Source of Peter's Eschatology

Note three passages from Peter that demonstrate that his eschatology was nothing but the hope of Israel.

Acts 3:21-24 -- Peter says that the "restoration of all things" to be completed at the *parousia* of Christ would be the fulfillment of all the prophets from Samuel forward, "yea, all who have ever written." Peter was not proclaiming a postponed hope of Israel. Nor did he proclaim a hope transferred to the church, taken away from Israel. He was not preaching an eschatological hope different from that promised to Israel.

1 Peter 1:3-12 – Peter was looking for the "ready to be revealed" salvation at Christ's coming. He specifically tells us that the Old Testament prophets foretold that salvation at the *parousia*. This certainly flies in the face of Butler's claim that the OT never predicted Christ's second coming. Furthermore, if we are sensitive to it, Peter's epistle is full of references to the Old Covenant last days prophecies.[83]

2 Peter 3:1-3, 13 – Peter informs us that his hope of the New Heaven and Earth at the Day of the Lord was "according to His promise" i.e. the Old Covenant promises found in the prophets who had spoken before.

---

[83] Indeed, the argument can be made that 1 Peter is concerned with demonstrating the fulfillment of God's OT promises to restore Israel. Peter makes it clear that he was anticipating the arrival of the salvation foretold in the OT prophets (1:9-12), and he repeatedly cites prophecies of the last days restoration of Israel (cf. 2:9-10). There can be no question about the source of Peter's eschatological hope.

There is virtually no disagreement among the commentators that Peter is citing, and even directly quoting from Isaiah's prediction of the New Creation. (There are other O.T. texts lying behind 2 Peter 3 such as Daniel 9 and Isaiah 50f, but Isaiah 65-66 are the ones that come most easily to mind).[84]

From these three texts from the pen of Peter it is easily established that his eschatological hope, his gospel, was nothing but the reiteration of the Old Testament promises made to Israel. For Peter then, there was an inextricable connection between *Torah and Telos*, between the fulfillment of the Law of Moses and the Day of the Lord.

☞ The Source of John's Eschatology

It is sometimes argued that John's gospel is not overly eschatological, because it contains no explicit statements such as, "The kingdom of heaven has drawn near," like Matthew and Mark. Also, whereas Matthew, Mark and Luke all contain parallel accounts of the Olivet Discourse, John's gospel is quiet about that account. However, this does not mean that John's gospel[85]– not to mention the Apocalypse– is not eschatological. Consider a few passages.

"Jesus said to her, 'Woman, believe Me, the hour is coming when you will neither on this mountain, nor in Jerusalem, worship the

---

[84] Interestingly, McDurmon, in an article on the New Creation, acknowledged that Peter was alluding to Isaiah 65, but then claimed that Isaiah was not, after all, the ultimate source of 2 Peter 3. Instead, Genesis 1f is the real source. On the one hand, McDurmon affirmed the fulfillment of 2 Peter 3, but, by claiming that Genesis serves as the real source, he was attempting to establish a yet future eschatology. This is untenable. 2 Peter was not both fulfilled and unfulfilled at the same time. McDurmon's article can be found on the American Vision website.

[85] When we speak of John's gospel, we are of course referring to his record of Jesus' words. Each of the eschatological passages cited herein came from the lips of Jesus. However, this does not negate–but rather reinforces-- the fact that John's gospel is about the fulfillment of God's promises to Israel.

50

Father. 22 You worship what you do not know; we know what we worship, for salvation is of the Jews. But the hour is coming, and now is, when the true worshipers will worship the Father in spirit and truth; for the Father is seeking such to worship Him'" (John 4:21f).

When understood *within its prophetic background and context*, this passage is tremendously eschatological. Jeremiah 3:14f had foretold the time– *when Israel was restored*– when men would no longer go to Jerusalem to worship.[86] The Ark of the Covenant would lose its covenantal significance.[87] The restoration of Israel is inseparably linked with the time of the kingdom, the coming of Messiah in judgment, resurrection and every other major eschatological tenet. So for Jesus to say that the hour had arrived when men would no longer worship in Jerusalem was to say that the time for Israel's salvation had come, the kingdom was near!

In chapter 5:24-28, Jesus spoke of the resurrection:

"Most assuredly, I say to you, the hour is coming, and now is, when the dead will hear the voice of the Son of God; and those who hear will live. For as the Father has life in Himself, so He has granted the Son to have life in Himself, and has given Him authority to execute judgment also, because He is the Son of Man.

---

[86] See also Malachi 1:12f, where YHVH promised that the time was coming in which He would have men to worship Him anywhere and everywhere. This implies that the geo-centric locus of worship would no longer be required.

[87] Jeremiah's statement that the Ark would no longer be "remembered" is incredibly important. The word "remembered" means significantly more than just brought to mental recollection. It means to be remembered *within a covenant context*. So, Jeremiah foretold the time when the Ark of the Covenant, the symbol of the Mosaic Covenant itself, would no longer retain that covenantal significance. Furthermore, note that Jeremiah likewise said that *the Ark would not be built again!* Well, if the Ark would not be built again, this infers, by logical necessity that the Ark was destroyed, *never to be rebuilt!* So much for all of the modern claims of the so-called re-discovery of the "lost Ark" hidden away in the foothills of Israel, or Ethiopia, or where ever.

Do not marvel at this; for the hour is coming in which all who are in the graves will hear His voice and come forth—those who have done good, to the resurrection of life, and those who have done evil, to the resurrection of condemnation."[88]

The prophetic background for Jesus' discourse here is Ezekiel 37 and Daniel 12. Both passages promised the resurrection of Israel, in the last days, at the end of the age and the establishment of the kingdom. There are of course other eschatological references in John, particularly to the resurrection. The resurrection was clearly the Old Covenant hope of Israel.

It should go without saying that John's Apocalypse is based squarely upon Israel's Old Testament promises. Virtually every scholar agrees that Revelation reiterates the prophecies of Daniel for instance. But, it is not only Daniel that John draws from. Revelation draws heavily from Isaiah, Zechariah, Ezekiel, and other Old Testament prophecies as well. John specifically tells us that the fulfillment of his vision would be when, "the mystery of God foretold by the prophets" would be fulfilled (Revelation 10:7).

It is a great theological tragedy when Bible students seek to understand, interpret and teach Revelation without an appreciation and

---

[88] Most exegetes see in John 5 two resurrections, one spiritual, one of corpses. Yet, there are not two resurrections disparate in nature, separated in time by what is now two millennia and counting. There was the *initiation* of the resurrection that had begun, and was awaiting *consummation*. This agrees perfectly well with the fact that in 1 Corinthians 15 Paul uses the *present passive indicative* to speak of the resurrection that was— when he wrote— *already in process*! See 1 Corinthians 15:35f. This hardly comports with the idea of corpses rising out of the ground. See Sam Frost's excellent treatment of 1 Corinthians 15, with emphasis on the present tenses. Sam Frost, *Exegetical Essays on the Resurrection of the Dead*, (Xenia, Ohio, TruthVoice Publishing, 2004)59f. Frost's book is available from me. Also, see Jack Scott's treatment of the present passive indicatives in 1 Corinthians at the 2008 Preterist Pilgrim Weekend. MP3s of Scott's presentations are available at www.eschatology.org.

understanding of the Old Testament background and source of Revelation. There is no possible way to properly understand and interpret Revelation without keeping it within its proper context and that is the fulfillment of God's promises to Israel. John's eschatological hope was nothing but the hope of Israel.

> **The failure to interpret Revelation as the final fulfillment of God's promises to Old Covenant Israel is a guarantee of a false interpretation of the book. The failure to honor this context of Revelation is surely one of the great theological failures of all**

☞ The Source of Paul's Eschatology

Paul was more than clear about the source and nature of his eschatology.

Acts 24:14-15: "But this I confess to you, that according to the Way which they call a sect, so I worship the God of my fathers, believing all things which are written in the Law and in the Prophets. I have hope in God, which they themselves also accept, that there will be a resurrection of the dead, both of the just and the unjust."

Acts 26:5f: "According to the strictest sect of our religion I lived a Pharisee. And now I stand and am judged *for the hope of the promise made by God to our fathers.* To this promise our twelve tribes, earnestly serving God night and day, hope to attain. For this hope's sake, King Agrippa, I am accused by the Jews. Why should it be thought incredible by you that God raises the dead?" (My emphasis)

Acts 26:21f: "Therefore, having obtained help from God, to this day I stand, witnessing both to small and great, *saying no other things than those which the prophets and Moses said would come*— that the Christ would suffer, that He would be the first to rise from the dead, and would proclaim light to the Jewish people and to the Gentiles."

Acts 28: 19f: "But when the Jews spoke against it, I was compelled to appeal to Caesar, not that I had anything of which to accuse my nation. For this reason therefore I have called for you, to see you and speak with you, because for the hope of Israel I am bound with this chain."

Romans 8:23-9:4: "Not only that, but we also who have the first-fruits of the Spirit, even we ourselves groan within ourselves, *eagerly waiting for the adoption*, the redemption of our body... I tell the truth in Christ, I am not lying, my conscience also bearing me witness in the Holy Spirit, 2 that I have great sorrow and continual grief in my heart. 3 For I could wish that I myself were accursed from Christ for my brethren, my countrymen according to the flesh, *4 who are Israelites, to whom pertain the adoption,* the glory, the covenants, the giving of the law, the service of God, and the promises."[89]

Now, if Paul said that his gospel, his eschatology, was *nothing* but what Moses and the prophets said, then this means that when we read Corinthians, Thessalonians, or any other of Paul's eschatological discourses, we are reading Paul's take on Israel's eschatological hope.

So, what we have established, beyond disputation, is that the one eschatological hope expressed by the NT writers was the fulfillment of God's Old Covenant promises made to Israel. They posited the eschatological consummation, not at the end of the Christian age, but, at the end of the age in which they were living, the Mosaic age.

As a closing note to this segment, we would note that the festal calendar of Israel indisputably demonstrates the *Torah Until Telos* motif and truth. That is, Israel's feast days, particularly the last three, foreshadowed the judgment, the completed Atonement and the resurrection. In addition, the Sabbath itself foreshadowed the final salvation and resurrection. I will be developing these concepts in another volume of this series, but wanted to introduce it here as "food for thought."

---

[89] See also Romans 16:25-26 also where Paul said that his gospel was drawn from the OT prophets. He is clear that what he preached was not "new" except in its unfolding. It had been there all along– in Israel's prophetic corpus– it simply had not been understood as it was being revealed through the apostles.

Here is the point of introducing this concept. There was nothing more intrinsically "Torah," more fundamentally, "the Law of Moses," than Israel's feast days and Sabbath (s). Yet, those feast days and Sabbath (s) were eschatological to the core. So, as Jesus said, "Not one jot or one tittle shall pass from the law, until it is all fulfilled." Since the feast days and Sabbath (s) were "the law" then until what they foretold was fully accomplished, not one jot or one tittle of Torah could pass. Nothing more clearly establishes the truth of *Torah until Telos* than this.

NOT ONE JOT OR ONE TITTLE SHALL PASS FROM "THE LAW..."
Defining "the law" in Matthew 5:17f

I have noted that attempts are made to avoid the power of Jesus' words in Matthew 5 by defining "the law" as something very narrowly defined, and not the entirety of the Old Law.

But, does the Bible carefully delineate between "the law" as moral code, versus ceremonial law, versus prophecy? Does the Bible use the term "the law" to refer to the Decalogue or even the Pentateuch, as opposed to the sacrificial code? The answer is a clear and unequivocal, *No!*

Before we proceed to define "the law" from scripture, it should be noted that there has traditionally been a strong consensus about the definition of Jesus' referent to "the law" in Matthew 5:17-18. However, what has happened over the last several years is that advocates of Covenant Eschatology, i.e. preterists, have begun to point out that:

A.) "The law" was in fact an inclusive, comprehensive term for the entirety of Torah.

B.) That Jesus said that not a single iota of "the law" could pass until it was all fulfilled.

C.) That "the law" is the source of all NT predictions of the eschatological consummation.

D.) That therefore, until all OT prophecies of the coming of the Lord, judgment and resurrection were fulfilled, not one jot or tittle of the law– inclusive of the sacrifices and feast days, would pass.

When confronted with this evidence, something radical and unprecedented has occurred. In the amillennial fellowship in which I was raised it was unheard of to dichotomize "the law" into different elements. Commentator after commentator affirmed the organic unity of Torah. "The law" was the Old Testament in its entirety, and there could be no compromise on this issue.

Now however, a brand new theology in regard to "the law" has arisen. Unknown arguments are being offered that just a few short years ago would never have been suggested. In fact, in formal debates against Sabbatarians, amillennial debaters have strongly condemned any attempt to dissect "the law" into disparate, unrelated, unconnected elements.

Let me illustrate what I am saying with some quotes from the leading amillennialists from my own former fellowship, as well as citations from other scholars who comment on the definition of "the law" as used in the NT. Some of these quotes were supplied by Tony Denton, who presented them in one of his lessons at the Preterist Pilgrim Weekend of 2011.[90]

Notice the following quotes.

J. W. McGarvey was one of the most prominent spokesman in the American Restoration movement of the late 19th century. His influence is still strong within that movement. He defined "the law": "The Old Testament generally is often called 'the Law' by New Testament writers."[91]

David Lipscomb was likewise an influential spokesman in the amillennial circles of the 19th century. He defined "the law": "The whole of the Old Testament Scripture is called 'the Law.'"[92]

Robert Taylor, a church of Christ minister made the following comments about the attempts to divide "the Law of Moses" or "the law":

> "A devilish device is sometimes resorted to by those who want to keep intact part of the Mosaic System with the remnant abrogated or abolished. They seek to make a distinction between the Law of God and the Law of Moses or between the moral law that God gave and the ceremonial law given by Moses. It all came wrapped up in the same package. It, at times, is called Moses' law; he

---

[90] The theme of the 2011 Preterist Pilgrim Weekend was "The Passing of Torah: At the Cross or AD 70?" DVDs and MP3s of that seminar are available from me through my websites.

[91] McGarvey, *Commentary on Thessalonians, Corinthians, Galatians, and Romans* by McGarvey & Pendleton, (The Restoration Library. Gospel Light Publishing Co.)139.

[92] David Lipscomb, *(A Commentary on the New Testament Epistles by Lipscomb & Shepherd: First Corinthians*, (Nashville, Gospel Advocate Co., 1984)210.

received it at Sinai. It, at times, is called the Law of God because He gave it at Sinai. The two are used interchangeably"[93]

Wayne Cox, amillennialist: "Though Sabbatarians attempt to make a distinction between moral and ceremonial law, and thus conclude the above texts to refer only to ceremonial law, Scripture makes no such distinction!"[94]

Jim McGuiggan, "The Law is the Old Testament."[95]

Mike Willis said, "Paul used the word 'Law' to refer to the entire Old Testament in this verse."; "The usage of the word *law (nomos)* in this verse is important. Some have contended that law is used exclusively for the Torah (Genesis -- Deuteronomy) because the canon of the Old Testament was incomplete. Others have maintained a division between various parts of the Old Testament for other reasons. However, Paul uses the word law to refer to the entire Old Testament in this verse (cf. its usage in John. 10:34; 15:25; Romans 3:19-20)."[96]

Mark Bailey (amillennialist): "'The 'Law' refers to the Old Testament.'"[97] Bailey was defining "the law" in Romans 3:19.

Quotes such as these from amillennialists could be multiplied many times over. Let me say again that the convictions expressed by these various commentators are the representative view in which I was personally raised. I am convinced these men have expressed the truth.

The problem is that, as noted above, there is a brand new theology being developed as a direct result of the preterist insistence on being

---

[93] Taylor, in a speech given at a lectureship in Mississippi. (The *Two Covenants*, Pulaski, Tn, Sain Publications, 1996)223.

[94] Wayne Cox, Mississippi Lectureship, (1996) 233f.

[95] Jim McGuiggan, *Looking Into the Bible Series. The Book of I Corinthians*, (Montex Publishing Co., 1984)182.

[96] Mike Willis, *Truth Commentaries. First Corinthians*, (Guardian of Truth Foundation, 1994)404.

[97] Mark Bailey, *Contending for the Faith. A Commentary on First Corinthians* by Wm. Mark Bailey. (Contending for the Faith Publications, 1994)502.

consistent with this truth in the light of what Jesus said in Matthew 5:17-18.

In the scholarly literature, there is really no debate about the definition of the term "the law" either in Matthew 5 or for that matter in Paul's epistles. For brevity sake, without giving a list of lengthy quotes, let me just give a list of the scholars that take note of the definition of the term "the law" in either Matthew 5:17 or in Paul's epistles, as referent to the entirety of the Old Law.

F. W. Grosheide,[98] Robertson & Plummer,[99] Charles Hodge,[100] Lenski,[101] G. K. Barrett,[102] Leon Morris.[103] These are but a few of the commentators who see the NT references, and particularly in the Pauline epistles, as referent to the entirety of the Old Testament.

In fact, when we consider Paul's epistles, it should be noted that per my count, he uses the term "the law" some 117 times. Unless he provides a contextual qualifier for his use of the term, as he does in

---

[98] *Grosheide, The International Commentary on the New Testament, The First Epistle to the Corinthians, (Grand Rapids,* Eerdmans, 1953)330.

[99] The International Critical Commentary, *A Critical and Exegetical Commentary of the First Epistle of St Paul to the Corinthians,* (Edinburgh, T & T Clark Ltd., 1986)316.

[100] Charles Hodge, *Commentary on the First Epistle to the Corinthians,* (Grand Rapids, Eerdmans, 1950)293. Hodge said, commenting on Paul's use of the term in 1 Corinthians 15: "Here, as in John 10:34, Rom. 3:20, and elsewhere, the reference is not to the Pentateuch, but to the Old Testament."

[101] R. C. H. Lenski, *The Interpretation of St. Paul's First and Second Epistles to the Corinthians,* (Augsburg Publishing House, 1937)599.

[102] *Harper's New Testament Commentaries. A Commentary on The First Epistle to the Corinthians,* (Hendrickson Publishers, 1968)322.

[103] Leon Morris, *Tyndale New Testament Commentaries. The First Epistle of Paul to the Corinthians,* (Grand Rapids, Eerdmans, 1985)192.

Romans 8:1-4, for instance, he refers invariably to Torah, the Law of Moses. As we shall see, this fact is a devastating critique and refutation of all futurist eschatologies that claim on the one hand that Torah has been abrogated, but, that the resurrection– foretold in "the law" has not yet been fulfilled.

In regard to Matthew 5, Hagner says: "The reference to 'the prophets' suggests that the significance of Jesus for the Mosaic Law can only be understood as part of a larger picture, namely the fulfillment of the entire Torah, understood in its broad sense, including the prophets. The entire OT can be referred to as 'the law and the prophets.'"[104]

Once again, this kind of documentation can easily be multiplied. The fact is that it has been, and continues to be, understood that the term "the law" when used without a contextual qualifier, was a term that encompassed the entirety of what we today call "the Old Testament" or even "the Mosaic Law." This is corroborated by the scriptures themselves.

Defining "The Law" From Scripture

When we examine the Biblical usage of the term "the law" there really is no doubt that it is commonly used in a comprehensive manner that falsifies the attempts to narrowly define the term in Matthew 5. We will offer here only a few examples that demonstrate this truth.

❖ In Deuteronomy 28-31, the term "the law," "the book of the law," "this book of the law," and similar terms are used.[105] The important thing to note is that Deuteronomy 28-31 is not only "the law" but, it is clearly prophetic (cf. 28:45f). In fact, it was prophetic of Israel's last days. Thus, these chapters, known as the Law of Blessings and Cursings, contain both moral mandates, covenantal provisions of blessings and cursings, as well as prophecy. Yet, no fine distinction between law and prophecy is made. It is simply called "the law."

Notice the following:

---

[104] Donald Hagner, *Word Biblical Commentary,* Matthew, Vol. #33a (Dallas, Tx., Word, 1995)108+.

[105] 28:61; 29:21; 30:10; 31:26; etc.

And there, in the presence of the children of Israel, he wrote on the stones a copy of the law of Moses, which he had written. Then all Israel, with their elders and officers and judges, stood on either side of the ark before the priests, the Levites, who bore the ark of the covenant of the LORD, the stranger as well as he who was born among them. Half of them were in front of Mount Gerazim and half of them in front of Mount Ebal, as Moses the servant of the LORD had commanded before, that they should bless the people of Israel. And afterward he read all the words of the law, the blessings and the cursings, according to all that is written in the Book of the Law (Joshua 8:32-34).

There could hardly be a clearer definition of "the law" than this.

The Law of Blessings and Cursings was "the law."

It was "the law of Moses."

It was "the book of the law."[106]

It was likewise the covenant.

Given how Joshua used these terms interchangeably, it is disingenuous to say the least that we must define "the law" in Matthew in a finely restricted way, i.e. "Moral commandments" or something else. To repeat an important point, there are no qualifiers in Matthew 5 that demand a limited definition of "the law." There are no restrictive comments, no defining statements about only certain elements of "the law" being in view.

✤ Jesus said, "the law and the prophets prophesied until John" (Luke 16:16). Thus, there was a prophetic element in even "the law" as far as

---

[106] The undeniable identification of the Law of Blessings and Cursings as "the law" will be important as we continue to develop our discussion of the passing of Torah in following volumes.

Jesus was concerned. The Law *prophesied*, and the prophets were "the law."

We should, perhaps point out that mandates such as, "thou shalt not steal" are pretty clearly not *prophetic*. This means that they can hardly fall under the rubric of "until all is fully accomplished" as Jesus demanded.[107]

I suggest that in Jesus' statement that "the law prophesied" he may well have been referring (at least) to the Pentateuch. As just noted, Deuteronomy is "the law" and Deuteronomy patently does prophesy. Furthermore, Jesus draws extensively from Deuteronomy in his ministry and message.

If this is what Jesus had in mind by "the law prophesied" then his statement in Matthew 5:17-18 about the absolute necessity for all of "the law" to be fulfilled before any of it could pass takes on added strength and confirms our thesis in this series. Here is why.

Deuteronomy 28-32 foretold Israel's last days. The Song of Moses– an essential part of "the law"– foretold the last days judgment of Israel when God would destroy her. And what cannot be missed, is that the last days judgment of Israel foretold in Deuteronomy 28-32 would be a direct result of *Israel's violation of Torah*, and, that destruction would be the ultimate and final outpouring of Mosaic Covenant wrath.

---

[107] In my written debate with Jerry McDonald he took the rather novel approach the when Jesus said the law and the prophets prophesied until John, that Jesus was not referring to *predictive* prophecy but simply to the teaching function of the law and the prophets. Thus, with the advent of John, the law and the prophets took on a new function or a new meaning. McDonald was taking a position virtually unknown in his fellowship, and while linguistically *possible* it is not supported by the text. John announced that "the kingdom of heaven has drawn near" and that means that whereas prophesy had foretold the "last days" arrival of the kingdom, that time had arrived. Very clearly, the foretelling aspect of the law is in view. McDonald was simply desperate to avoid this truth.

So, Jesus' statement that "the law prophesied" demands that we look closely at the definition of "the law"since, once again, the Ten Commandments, with the exception of Sabbath,[108] *did not prophesy.*

Now, take note of the fact that the Sabbath, *which was undoubtedly prophetic* was embedded firmly in "the law" i.e. the Decalogue. This would naturally allow Jesus to say "the law prophesied." No Jew would ever, not for one moment, believe that a distinction was to be made between "the law" of the moral mandates, and "the law" i.e. the prophetic element of the Sabbath. Such a distinction is unknown in Jewish thought.

✤ In one of Jesus' controversies with the Jews, they said, "We have heard from the law that the Christ remains forever; and how can You say, 'The Son of Man must be lifted up'? Who is this Son of Man?" (John 12:34).

Now, the Law, i.e. the moral mandates of Decalogue, as defined by those who seek to avoid the comprehensive definition of Torah, contains no such thing as Messiah remaining forever. That concept is found in the Psalms and in the prophets (cf. Psalms 89; Isaiah 6:9f). But, for the Jews of Jesus' day, there was clearly no definition of "the law" that excluded the Psalms and the prophets. Thus, "the law" was "the psalms and the prophets" and that means that until every jot and every tittle found in the law and the prophets came to realization, none of Torah would pass.

✤ In John 15:25 Jesus spoke of the unbelief of the Jews and their hatred of him. He said: "This happened that the word might be fulfilled which is written in their law, 'They hated me without a cause.'"

Jesus quotes from Psalms 69, and he calls it "their law." So, the Psalms were, as just seen, "the law."

Note also that Jesus said that the Jew's unbelief "fulfilled" what was predicted. We have here a clear-cut definition of what Jesus meant by

---

[108] We will be discussing the Sabbath and Israel's festal calendar in another volume in this series. Suffice it to say for now that those who insist that Torah passed at the cross are grossly ignoring or overlooking the issue of the Sabbath and the feast days.

"the law" and what he meant by "fulfill." Jesus' usage of the term "the law" in chapter 12 and 15 to refer to predictive prophecy falsifies the objection noted above, that when Jesus said "the law and the prophets prophesied until John" that he was not speaking of predictive prophecy. Very clearly, the Psalms and Isaiah were prophetic– not just "instructive"– of events in Jesus' ministry. Thus, the law did indeed continue to "foretell" after John.

❖ As Paul was on trial, he gave his defense against the Pharisees seeking his life for his views on the resurrection:

"But this I confess to you, that according to the Way which they call a sect, so I worship the God of my fathers, believing all things which are written in the Law and in the Prophets. I have hope in God, which they themselves also accept, that there will be a resurrection of the dead, both of the just and the unjust."

Notice that Paul said he believed in, "the law and the prophets" and that the law and the prophets foretold the resurrection. Now, if we are to make a sharp distinction between moral mandates and prophecy, we must confront Paul's terminology. As far as Paul was concerned, "the law" foretold the resurrection and was the source of his resurrection doctrine and hope. This patently falsifies any attempt to dichotomize between "the law" and "the prophets."

Where in the Decalogue, (The Ten Commandments) or the "moral mandates" do we find the hope and prophecy of the resurrection? It is not in "thou shalt not steal" or, "thou shalt not commit adultery." It is, however, right there under everyone's nose, *in the typological meaning of the Sabbath.*

The Sabbath anticipated the "final salvation", did it not? As Kurtz says, "The earthly Sabbath reflected the Sabbath of God after the creation was finished – a Sabbath in which man, beast, and field participated, in the fulness of their native glory, and the blessedness before the Fall. And as every repristination of the lost blessing of creation, however transient, is at the same time a typical anticipation of their future restoration, the blessedness of the Sabbath rest, enjoyed

64

by man, beast, and field, was a typical pledge and prophecy of the rest of the lat time."[109]

Edersheim says that according to the ancients the Sabbath anticipated "that final Messianic Kingdom," and, "ultimately to the eternal Sabbath of completed redemption, and completed 'hallowing' (Revelation 11)."[110]

Notice Edersheim's referent to Revelation 11, which of course is a prediction of the resurrection at the sounding of the seventh trump. And don't forget that in Israel's festal calendar the sounding of the trumpets announced the arrival of Sabbath and the Sabbaths. Goppelt says of the Sabbath: "The Sabbath is interpreted as an eschatological type more than any other OT institution"[111] *The Dictionary of Biblical Imagery* says that the Sabbath is depicted in Hebrews 4 as "heaven itself."[112]

In my debate with Jerry McDonald, I asked the following:
<1.) Scripture said that the New Moons, Feast Days and Sabbaths of Israel's festal calendar were "shadows of good things to come" (Colossians 2:14-17; Hebrews 9:6f; 10:1-3). What did the following feast days foreshadow and typify:
Feast of Trumpets (Rosh Ha Shanah).
McDonald's Answer: The Final Judgment.
Day of Atonement– **Answer**: The Day of Salvation.
Feast of Harvest / Booths -- **Answer**: The Resurrection.

---

[109] J. H. Kurtz, *Sacrificial Worship of the Old Testament*, (Grand Rapids, Baker, 1980)344.

[110] Alfred Edersheim, *The Temple: Its Ministry and Services*, (Updated Edition, Peabody, Mass., 2004)134+.

[111] Leonard Goppelt, Typos, *The Typological Interpretation of the Old Testament in the New* (Grand Rapids, Eerdmans, 1982)37.

[112] *Dictionary of Biblical Imagery*, Editors Leland Ryken, James Wilhoit, Tremper Longman III, (Downers Grove, Ill., 1998)747.

2.) What did the seventh day Sabbath and the other festal Sabbaths foreshadow, and has that which the Sabbath (Sabbaths) foreshadowed been completely fulfilled? **Answer**: Heaven (Heb. 4:9-11).>

What is so interesting about McDonald's answer is that he gave these answers in an initial draft of his second negative. However, he shortly withdrew that version and sent another, revised version of his second negative, and then a third. In his final response *he deleted all references to my questions!*

McDonald's answers typify the confusion in much of the theological world in regard to Torah and the feast days / Sabbath issue. It is widely acknowledged that the Sabbath typified final salvation and Trumpets represented judgment. The Day of Atonement represented salvation. The Feast of Harvest represented the resurrection. In an ensuing volume we will discuss this critical issue in-depth.

The question is, how in the name of reason and sound logic can one affirm that Torah, all of Torah, was annulled at the cross, as all three futurist eschatologies do to varying degrees, and then affirm that the Day of Judgment, final salvation and the resurrection, all in fulfillment of Rosh Ha Shanah, Atonement and the Feast of Harvest, are yet future? This is patently wrong.

If the eschatological feast days have not been fulfilled then they stand valid, as shadows of things yet to come. But, if those feast days are not fulfilled *then the entirety of Torah remains*, for "not one jot or one tittle of the Law shall pass until it is all fulfilled."

McDonald sought to avoid the power of these indisputable facts by inventing a brand new doctrine. He claimed that although the resurrection was indeed foreshadowed and promised "in the law" that in reality, the resurrection promise was "not part of the law." He based his claim on the fact that Job, who preceded Torah, foretold the resurrection. As I noted in response, based on such "logic" one could argue that animal sacrifices were not actually "of the law" since they clearly antedated Torah itself.[113]

---

[113] I likewise took note that in the amillennial world of McDonald, his argument is unprecedented. I presented a chart with quotes from numerous prominent ministers from his fellowship, all of whom defined "the law" as the entirety of the Old Testament. Many of those quotes are given above as well.

The indisputable fact is that many things that were incorporated into Torah *predated Sinai*. Circumcision predated Torah, but was certainly part of Torah. Animal sacrifice pre-dated the Law of Moses, but was indubitably an intrinsic part of the law. Even the Sabbath was observed by Israel prior to the codification of that law (Exodus 16).

So, to suggest that because something predated the Law of Moses, means it was not incorporated into the Law, and was not part of the Law, is specious to say the least. Sabbath was part of the Law and Sabbath foreshadowed the resurrection. It was necessary for the typological and prophetic elements of those things to be accomplished for Torah to pass.

The suggestion that the resurrection was not an integral part of the law is surely one of the most disingenuous "arguments" I have personally encountered. It exemplifies the desperation of the "anti-preterist" world to find some argument, *any argument*, to counter Jesus' words: "Not one jot or one tittle shall pass from the law until it is all fulfilled."

It should be noted at this juncture that Paul agreed that prophecy was "the law." In 1 Corinthians 14:21-22, Paul, seeking to correct the abuses of the charismata among the Corinthians, had this to say:

"In the law it is written: 'With men of other tongues and other lips I will speak to this people; And yet, for all that, they will not hear Me,' says the Lord. Therefore tongues are for a sign, not to those who believe but to unbelievers; but prophesying is not for unbelievers but for those who believe."

Paul is quoting directly from Isaiah 28:11, which of course, is in turn, echoing Deuteronomy 28– the Law of Blessings and Cursings. Paul's citation of Isaiah as "the law" shows that in his mind, one could not sharply divide Torah into distinct, unrelated aspects. Patently, for Paul, Isaiah was "the law." If Paul the inspired apostle called Isaiah "the law" then it is wrong for moderns to deny that the prophets were the law.

The debate is on both my websites. McDonald agreed that his view was not the traditional view, but refused to give textual support for his claims.

2.) Jesus said he came to fulfill the law and the prophets. He did not come to fulfill the law divorced from the prophets.[114]

3.) Jesus said not one iota would pass from the law and the prophets until it was all fully accomplished (*from genetai – more on this below*). The word *genetai*, not *pleroma* as used earlier in the verse, is significant and we will have more to say on it below. For now, notice what Paul said of the resurrection prophecies from the OT.

In 1 Corinthians 15 the apostle said that the resurrection would be when "the law" would be *accomplished (from genetai)* when "the law" that was "the strength of sin" was removed (v. 55-56).

Thus, the law would stand until it's mission was accomplished– at the resurrection. The law would have served its purpose when all that it foretold was fully accomplished. With its purpose fulfilled, completely accomplished, then and only then would Torah pass away.

So, we have demonstrated that the term "the law" is a comprehensive term used by the ancients. The Old Testament itself referred to all aspects of the Law of Moses simply as "the law." Jesus and his apostles likewise speak of the entire corpus of Torah, the Decalogue, the Pentateuch, the prophets. It is not too much to say that no part of the Old Testament is ever not called "the law."

This truth falsifies the modern attempts to say that some of the Law would be fulfilled and then some of the law would pass, while some of the law will remain until the so called "end of time." This is an open violation of Jesus' words and should be abandoned. His words should resound in our ears and hearts: "Not one jot or one tittle shall pass from the law until it is all fulfilled."

---

[114] Below, we will take note of the objection that Jesus' claim that he *came*, i.e. his incarnation, to fulfill, this falsifies the idea that the eschatological promises of Torah had to be fulfilled for the law to pass. The objection fails to honor the Biblical fact that he came to fulfill, and, he was coming, his parousia, *to fulfill all things* (Acts 3:23f). It is, therefore, too atomistic to claim that his incarnation was all that was necessary to fulfill all things.

The indisputable fact is that all of modern evanglical Christianity is in direct violation of Jesus' words.

He said not one jot or one tittle would pass from the law until every jot and every tittle was fulfilled.

Modern Christianity says some of Torah was fulfilled, and some of Torah passed away, but, an awful lot of the jots and tittles of the Law of Moses remain in effect, and will remain in force until the supposed "end of time."

This is patently not what Jesus said.

So, Jesus' words seem clear and unambiguous– not a single particle of Torah, not the crossing of a "T" or the dotting of an "I" would pass until every single thing anticipated in Israel's covenant with YHVH came to pass. Yet, in historical Christianity, these simple words have been and continue to be troublesome, to say the very least.

The fact is that modern Christianity does not accept Jesus' words. I know that sounds like a strong statement, and it is. It is intended to be so. But the statement is indisputably true. Here is why.

Evangelical Christianity still believes that Torah, in varying degrees, remains valid, while claiming to believe that the Law of Moses has passed away. That is contradictory, you say? Yes, it is, and is a clear violation of Jesus' words. He did not say "When some has been fulfilled, then some will pass." Yet, that is precisely the view held by the majority of Bible students today.

As we documented above, all three futurist views of eschatology posit the end of the Law of Moses in the first century. However, they then turn around and appeal to "the Law" for either their ecclesiological functions (Sabbatarianism, with its dietary laws), or their eschatological doctrine, e.g. dispensationalism, which depends most heavily on the OT for support.

Thomas Ice, dispensationalist, as we have noted, claims to believe that the law of Moses was completely fulfilled and removed in the first century. However, he then turns around and claims: "As significant as

Deuteronomy 4 is (which he calls Israel's "prophetic roadmap for the future," dkp) in establishing the Tribulation and its purpose, an expanded narrative of Israel's future history is provided in Deuteronomy 28-32." He then cites David Larsen, 'The last seven chapters of Deuteronomy (28-34) are really the matrix out of which the great prophecies of the Old Testament regarding Israel emerge."[115]

Okay, so on the one hand, the law of Moses has been fulfilled and removed, but on the other hand the law of Moses remains valid as the prophetic roadmap for the future. To say that this is self-contradictory is an understatement of huge proportion.

But the dispensationalists are not alone in their confusion over the Law of Moses. As we have seen above, postmillennialists likewise claim to believe that God has abrogated certain parts (some jots and tittles) of Torah– i.e. the ceremonial, sacrificial, cultic aspects, while maintaining that we are still looking for the fulfillment of God's OT covenant with Israel at the end of human history (Romans 11:25-27). And then of course, as we have shown, one of the foundational tenets of amillennialism is that Torah ended at the Cross, and God no longer had any covenant relationship with Israel from that time.

While each of the futurist views claims to believe that Torah has been annulled in Christ, nonetheless, they all posit the abiding validity of some of the Law of Moses, i.e. the prophetic element, or the Sabbath.[116] But what this means, without any dispute, is that all three eschatologies are thereby saying that some jots and tittles have passed, but, some jots and tittles have not passed. This is an unequivocal denial of Jesus' words.

So, how do futurist commentators seek to avoid what seems to be such a flagrant violation of Jesus words? Well, they all tell us, in different ways, *that Jesus did not mean what he said.* They tell us that

---

[115] Thomas Ice in, *The Great Tribulation Past or Future, a written debate* with Ken Gentry, (Grand Rapids, Kregel, 1999)75, 76.

[116] The Sabbatarians deny that the Sabbath was part of "the law of Moses" insisting instead that it was "the law of God." As we shall see below, this is a false distinction without Biblical merit.

Jesus did not mean that all of the Law of Moses had to be fulfilled, only part of it.

In addition to what we have already presented, let me lay before the reader the "explanations" that I have encountered over the years, both in formal public debate, in numerous written debates, and in countless private studies and discussions.

1.) Jesus only meant to say that *when the Law had fulfilled its purpose* it would pass. He was not saying that all of Torah had to be fulfilled. (Doesn't this say that the parts that were unfulfilled, did not have a purpose?)

2.) Jesus was referring to the cultic practices passing away, when he would fulfill the typology of the sacrificial system in his death.

3.) The Bible affirms that Jesus did fulfill all things when he died on the cross (Luke 18; 24).

4.) Related to #2, it is claimed that "the Law" in Matthew 5:17-18 refers to the cultic, sacrificial element of Torah, but has nothing to do with the Decalogue, i.e. the moral law.[117]

5.) Jesus said, "I did not come to destroy, but to fulfill." This is taken to mean that Jesus' personal ministry was all that was necessary to fulfill "every jot and every tittle."

6.) Since Jesus said that Torah would not pass away until the heaven and earth passes, this means that the Law remains valid– particularly the Decalogue (and Sabbath)– until the "end of time." (Sabbatarianism and Theonomists).

---

[117] This claim is problematic for the Sabbatarians who normally claim that the term "the law" is referent to the Decalogue, and not the cultic, ceremonial laws. By identifying "the law" in Matthew as the Decalogue, the Sabbatarians seek to avoid the passing of Sabbath, but, inadvertently imply that the ceremonial cultus was fulfilled and passed– thus demanding fulfilled eschatology!

7.) Related to points # 2 and 4, it is often argued that the prophetic element of the Old Law was not in fact "the law." So, "the law" is dichotomized into "the law" (moral mandates by some, ceremonial commands by others[118]) and then the rest of the Old Testament.

When we look at each of these objections, it is clear that there is massive misunderstanding of the definition of "the law" in evangelical Christianity. What I want to do now is to look even closer at the definition of "the law."

I maintain that the proper definition of "the law" as used in Scripture makes it impossible to sustain the modern evangelical attempts to divide Torah into distinctive elements unrelated to one another, in which some elements were "the law" while some elements were not.

---

[118] It will be quickly seen that if one calls the "ceremonial laws" concerning the feast days and animal sacrifices "the law" then patently, all that those festal, sacrificial mandates foreshadowed had to be fully accomplished for Torah, any of it, to pass. Realizing this, some now say that *some* of "the law" i.e. the cultic commands were removed, but, the Decalogue– which of course contained the typological Sabbath– remains valid. However, they then say that all of the Decalogue remains valid, *except the Sabbath!* This is the position now taken by Kurt Simmons,. See our written debate: *The Passing of Torah: At the Cross or AD 70.* So, once again, this means that some of the Law would pass when some of it was fulfilled, in direct violation of Jesus' words.

BIBLICALLY DEFINING "THE LAW"

What was the Law? What was simply "the Law" from the Jewish and Biblical perspective!

While we have already addressed these questions somewhat, I want to look a bit closer at the Biblical evidence

So, once again, what was considered and called "the law" by the Jews, by scripture, by Jesus and the NT authors?

THE PENTATEUCH AS A WHOLE
WAS CALLED THE LAW

Let me make one observation here before we begin our investigation in-depth. There is no question that there are different genres of literature in the Old Covenant. No one denies that the legalistic commands found in Exodus, Leviticus, Numbers and Deuteronomy are different in form from Chronicles, or Samuel, or the Psalms or Isaiah. *Form and genre are not the issue.* The issue is, were these different genres of literature considered authoritative, and were they called the law by the ancient writers, the Jews, Jesus and his disciples.

When one surveys the Old Testament as well as the New, they will discover that there is no sharp discrimination in the Jewish vernacular in regard to what they called the law. The term is used literally hundreds of times, and has a comprehensive aspect to it.

The Pentateuch And Decalogue Were Called The Law

I am not going to spend space documenting what is incontrovertible and undisputed. To my knowledge, no one has denied that the Pentateuch, the first five books of the Old Testament, were called "the law." This is extremely important as we shall see, but I will leave that further discussion for below.

We will, however examine below the Sabbatarian claim that the Bible distinguishes between "law of Moses" and "the law of God." For now, we will accept as universally agreed that the Pentateuch was called "the law." Adventists and Sabbatarians insist on this distinction, claiming that the law of Moses, i.e. the ceremonial and sacrificial system, has been annulled, while the moral mandates of the Decalogue remain binding.

Likewise, I am not going to spend time or space establishing what is also accepted in all circles, and that is that the *Decalogue* was called "the law" by the Jews. Once again, there is no dispute or controversy about this. But, look briefly at what this means:

The Pentateuch and the Decalogue were "the law."

But, not one jot or one tittle would pass from "the law" i.e. the Pentateuch and the Decalogue, until it was all fulfilled.

Therefore, not one jot or one tittle would pass from the Pentateuch or the Decalogue until every jot and every tittle contained in the Pentateuch and the Decalogue was all fulfilled.

Since no one that I am aware of has ever denied that the Pentateuch and the Decalogue were "the law" the only thing that truly needs to be established is whether the Psalms and the Prophets were called and considered to be "the law." If they were, then when Jesus said that not one jot or one tittle of the law would pass until it was all fulfilled, this demands that all prophecy contained in the Psalms and the prophets (the law) had to be fully accomplished before any of the Torah could pass.

The Psalms Were Called The Law

✣ We have already noted this, but it is important to reiterate. As Jesus was confronted by the Jews, they said, "We have heard from the law that the Christ remains forever; and how can You say, 'The Son of Man must be lifted up'? Who is this Son of Man?" (John 12:34).

As we have seen, the Law, i.e. the moral mandates of Decalogue, as defined by those who seek to avoid the comprehensive definition of Torah, contains no such thing as Messiah remaining forever. That concept is found in the Psalms and in the prophets (cf. Psalms 89; Isaiah 6:9f). But, for the Jews of Jesus' day, there was clearly no definition of "the law" that excluded the Psalms and the prophets. Thus, "the law" was "the psalms and the prophets" and that means that until every jot and every tittle found in the law and the prophets came to realization, none of Torah would pass.

✣ Paul likewise quotes from the Psalms no less than seven times in Romans 3:11-18, and says, "we know that whatever the law says, it

74

says to those under the law" (Romans 3:19). Thus, for Paul, the Psalms were "the law."

So, we have Paul, a rabbinically trained Jew intimately familiar with the *Sitz em leben* (the real life situation) of the first century Jewish thought, and he refers to both the Psalms and the prophetic corpus as "the law."

Back to the Pentateuch

I mentioned above that no one denies that the Pentateuch, Genesis-Deuteronomy, was called "the law." This is axiomatic and undeniable. However, most Bible students do not stop to consider the implications of that admission in light of Matthew 5:17-18.

As we have noted above, Thomas Ice says on the one hand that the law of Moses was forever removed by Christ. However, while he claims that the law of Moses– and he considers Deuteronomy to be part of the law of Moses – he then calls Deuteronomy God's prophetic roadmap for yet future events concerning Israel.[119] This is a glaring inconsistency and fatal to Ice's eschatology. But, the fact that Deuteronomy (and the Pentateuch) is incontrovertibly called and considered to be "the law" gives all futurists equal difficulties.

Let me illustrate this by examining the story of John the Baptizer.[120] John the Baptizer was:

☞ *The Voice* of one crying in the wilderness to prepare for the coming of the Lord in judgment and the kingdom, in fulfillment of Isaiah 40.1-12 (Mark 1:1-3).

---

[119] Thomas Ice in, *The Great Tribulation Past or Future, a written debate* with Ken Gentry, (Grand Rapids, Kregel, 1999)75, 76.

[120] This material is but a sketch of another volume planned in this series on the relationship between John the Immerser as Elijah, and the passing of Torah. This greatly overlooked connection is definitive proof that the law of Moses did not pass away at the cross. I presented some of this material in my debate with Jerry McDonald. The material confused him so badly that he responded by claiming on the one hand that Malachi did *not* predict AD 70, but then, just a few paragraphs later, insisted that Malachi *did* foretell AD 70!

☛ *The Messenger* to prepare the way for the coming of the Lord in judgment (Malachi 3:1-5).

☛ *Elijah*, who was prepare the way for the coming of the Great and Terrible Day of the Lord (Malachi 4:5-6– Matthew 17:10-12).

Notice now that Malachi 3:1-5 foretold the coming of the Lord in judgment of the sorcerer, the perjurer, the adulterer, those who mistreated the widows and the orphans, and who denied the Gentiles their proper kingdom privileges.

In my personal experience, I have found lamentably few Bible students who see the incredible implications of these facts and connections. A bit of explication is in order.

Each of the sins listed in Malachi 3.5 are based directly on Torah, the law of Moses, the Pentateuch, and in principle, even the Decalogue. Note Exodus 22.21-24:

"You shall neither mistreat a stranger nor oppress him, for you were strangers in the land of Egypt. You shall not afflict any widow or fatherless child. If you afflict them in any way, and they cry at all to Me, I will surely hear their cry; and My wrath will become hot, and I will kill you with the sword; your wives shall be widows, and your children fatherless."

Likewise, in Deuteronomy 27.19: "Cursed is the one who perverts the justice due the stranger, the fatherless, and widow.' 'And all the people shall say, 'Amen!'"

So, what we have in Malachi 3 is the prediction that the Lord was coming in judgment to impose the covenantal sanctions of Exodus and Deuteronomy, i.e. what every one freely calls the Law of Moses. According to Exodus those sanctions included invasion and death by the sword. This is nationalistic and corporate judgment.

It is indisputably true, of course, that if a law or covenant has been annulled, that all provisions found in that now dead covenant are no longer valid and applicable. This axiomatic truth cannot be refuted or denied. It is simply common sense. A dead covenant is, well, dead![121]

---

[121] In spite of this undeniable truth, in my written debate with Kurt Simmons he claimed that the provisions of a dead law / covenant can be enforced and applied! When I challenged him to provide even one legal example of this, he was, naturally, totally silent. The very idea that such could be

Here is what this fundamental truth, applied to Malachi's prediction, means. Malachi predicted the coming of the Lord in the application of the Law of Moses Covenantal wrath. Thus, the coming of the Lord foretold by Malachi would have to be fulfilled while the law of Moses, with those covenantal sanctions, was still binding. But let's see what that means in regard to John.

Remember, John was the messenger who was to prepare the people for the coming of the Lord in the application of those Mosaic Covenant sanctions. Here is where the "rub" for the traditional views of Torah comes into play.

As we have seen, all futurist eschatologies say that the law of Moses was done away with at the cross. But, if the law of Moses was abrogated at the cross, then when did the Great Day of the Lord, that John was heralding, take place? When did the Lord come in judgment, in application of Mosaic Covenant wrath, in fulfillment of Malachi, *after John* but before the cross, where those sanctions were supposedly annulled?

If the Lord did not come in fulfilment of Malachi's prophecy and the work of John, then Malachi's prophecy failed and both he and John were false prophets.

Very clearly, historically, the Lord did not come in judgment of Israel for violating Exodus and Deuteronomy, in the interim period between John the Baptizer and the cross. It simply did not happen, and I know of no one that claims that He did. In fact, comparatively speaking, that 3 ½ year period of time was relatively peaceful. But, one thing is certain, John most assuredly taught that the judgment he was heralding was near!

---

true is ludicrous, and exemplifies Simmons' desperation. That debate is in book form: *The End of Torah: At the Cross or AD 70*, and is available from my websites, Amazon, and other retailers.

John, as the messenger of Malachi 3, was to herald the coming of the Lord in the application of *Mosaic Covenant Wrath against Israel*.

The Law of Moses supposedly died at the cross.

But, if Torah died at the cross, then Malachi's prophecy had to have been fulfilled after John, but before the cross.

Clearly, the Lord did not come in wrath against Israel from the time of John until the cross, when Torah supposedly died.

Thus, the prophecy of Malachi failed or John lied!

Or....

Torah did not pass at the cross, since the Lord did come in judgment of Israel in AD 70!

John and Judgment– The End is Near

The failure to appreciate John as the messenger of Malachi 3-4 has tremendous implications for not only a person's view of the passing of Torah, but, of eschatology as a whole.

As we have noted just above, John was *The Voice, The Messenger* and *Elijah*. He was the sign and the herald of the Great and Terrible Day of the Lord. He was not the sign and herald of Jesus' incarnation. Neither Isaiah 40, Malachi 3 or chapter 4 can be construed as referent to Jesus' incarnation, in which he was the Suffering Servant, who would not bruise a reed, or extinguish a smoking flax (Isaiah 42) because of his humility. Each of these prophecies is about the coming of the Lord *in judgment in application of Mosaic Covenant wrath.*

As the herald and sign of the Great Day of the Lord, John's message was clear and unmistakable: Judgment was near. The language of Matthew 3 is too emphatic, too unambiguous.

Notice that John challenged the Pharisees and Sadducees: "Who has warned you to flee from the wrath (about) to come?"

Incidentally, there is something here about John's audience that should grab our attention as to the nature of the Day of the Lord being proclaimed by John. Was he predicting the "end of time" when the entire cosmos would be destroyed, and all men receive their reward in either heaven or hell? Many commentators take the position. However, this is untenable. Notice that the *Sadducees* were coming to John to be baptized by him, in order to flee from "the wrath about to come." Who are the Sadducees?

Josephus tells us that the Sadducees:

"The Pharisees are those who are esteemed most skillful in the exact explication of their laws. [...] They ascribe all to Fate and to God, and yet allow that to act what is right, or the contrary, is principally in the power of men, although Fate does co-operate in every action. They say that all souls are incorruptible, but that the souls of good men only are removed into other bodies and that the souls of bad men are subject to eternal punishment.

But the Sadducees [...] take away Fate entirely, and suppose that God is not concerned in our doing or not doing what is evil; and they say, that to act what is good, or what is evil, is at men's own choice, and that the one or the other belongs so to every one, that they may act as they please. They also take away the belief of the immortal duration of the soul, and the punishments and rewards in the Underworld."[122]

Likewise, Luke, recording Paul on trial before the Pharisees and Sadducees, offers this:

"When Paul perceived that one part were Sadducees and the other Pharisees, he cried out in the council, 'Men and brethren, I am a Pharisee, the son of a Pharisee; concerning the hope and resurrection of the dead I am being judged!' And when he had said this, a dissension arose between the Pharisees and the Sadducees; and the assembly was divided. For Sadducees say that there is no resurrection, and no angel or spirit; but the Pharisees confess both. Then there arose a loud outcry. And the scribes of the Pharisees' party arose and protested, saying, 'We find no evil in this man; but if a spirit or an angel has spoken to him, let us not fight against God." Acts 23:6-9)

So, in essence, the Sadducees rejected the idea of an afterlife. They rejected the idea that man will receive an "eternal reward" either in heaven or hell. So, that raises a serious question.

---

[122] Flavius Josephus, Jewish War 2.162-166.

If the Sadducees did not believe in a Day of the Lord that would result in "final judgment" of receiving eternal life or condemnation, why were they going out to John to be baptized by him, in order to escape the impending Day of the Lord? If they do not believe in heaven, were they simply "swearing that there ain't no heaven, but praying that there ain't no hell", to borrow a line from a popular rock song of a few years back?

The fact that the Sadducees were coming to John to flee from the wrath about to come is highly suggestive, if not determinative, that the impending Day of the Lord was to be a nationalistic judgment, and not the time ending, earth burning, final judgment commonly posited by the commentators. After all, Biblically, the Day of the Lord in Israel's history had always been an in-time, nationalistic catastrophe, when YHVH brought a foreign nation against her. Those judgments were invariably due to her violation of Torah, *which is precisely what Malachi 3 predicted, and John proclaimed.*[123]

Hagner notes:

"John's apocalyptic message invoked an imminent judgment of the unrighteous in (*tes mellouses orges*) 'the coming wrath.' This eschatological wrath, associated with the fulfillment is further alluded to in vv. 10-12. Abundant parallels indicate that this was a fixed component of Jewish apocalyptic expectation (see esp. Daniel 7:9-11; Isaiah 13:9; Zephaniah 1:15; 2:2-3; Malachi 4:1). The construction (*phugein* with *apo*) is a Hebraism (BDF §149). What frightened John's listeners was the insistence that the judgment was about to occur (*mellouses*). The fleeing (as from a burning field) is particularly appropriate to the figurative mention of vipers. (For notion of coming wrath in the early church see 1 Thessalonians 1:10; Ephesians 5:6; Colossians 3:6)."[124]

---

[123] See my *Like Father Like Son, On Clouds of Glory,* for an extended discussion of the Day of the Lord throughout the Bible. The Day of the Lord was never a time ending, earth burning event, as most modern Bible students believe.

[124] Donald Hagner, *Word Biblical Commentary, Vol. 33a,* (Dallas, Word, 1993)50.

Likewise, *Alford's Greek Testament* comments on John's message, "John is now speaking in the true character of a prophet, foretelling the wrath soon to be poured out on the Jewish nation."[125]

It is impossible to read Matthew 3 and miss the sense of urgency, of imminency in John's message. The wrath that he foretold, as Elijah, was "about to come" (v. 7). When John says, "the axe is already at the root" this is a direct allusion back to Malachi 4:1f where the Day of the Lord would leave "neither root nor branch." The burning of the chaff likewise hearkens back to Malachi 4 and the burning of the stubble with fire on the Great Day of the Lord. John's statement that the "winnowing fork is in his hand" cannot be extrapolated or extended millennia into the future. John, as Elijah, was warning Israel that the Great and Terrible Day of the Lord was near; they needed to repent!

While much, much more could be written about John as Elijah,[126] the herald of the Great and Terrible Day of the Lord, let me make my point about the passing of Torah.

To drive home the point about John's relationship to the passing of Torah, let me reiterate the material from above, and offer a few more relevant comments.

John the Baptizer was the Voice, the Messenger and Elijah as foretold in Isaiah 40 and Malachi 3 and 4. Of this there can be no doubt or dispute.

As the Voice, the Messenger and Elijah, John was to prepare the way for the coming of the Lord.

---

[125] *Henry Alford's Greek Testament,* Vol. 1, (Grand Rapids, Baker, 1980)22.

[126] I have been, for the last few years, writing a book on the eschatological significance of John as Elijah. It is truly sad to realize how little attention John receives. After his death in Matthew 14, commentators all but dismiss him and his message as relevant to Jesus' continuing ministry, or to the rest of the NT corpus and the eschatological message. This is a horrible oversight, and fails to realize that John's message is all but determinative for understanding NT eschatology. As noted above, in another volume in this series, I intend to present a good deal of material on John as an eschatological figure.

81

The coming of the Lord that John was to proclaim and prepare the people for, was the coming of the Lord in judgment. John's message about the coming of the Lord was not about the incarnation of Jesus.

The coming of the Lord that John was to proclaim was the coming of the Lord in judgment of Israel for violation of Torah (Malachi 3:1-5; 4:4-6). The sins delineated there are directly from the Pentateuch (Exodus 22:19-22; Deuteronomy 29:17f), i.e. "The law."

John, as Elijah, said the judgment that he was proclaiming was near. Thus, the Great and Terrible Day of the Lord was near.

This means that the coming of the Lord in the application of *Mosaic Covenant Wrath against Israel* was near.

The Law of Moses supposedly died at the cross.

But, if Torah died at the cross, then Malachi's prophecy had to have been fulfilled *after John, but before the cross.*

The indisputable fact is that the Lord did not come in wrath against Israel in the application of Mosaic Covenant sanctions, from the time of John until the cross, when Torah supposedly died.

So, where ever you place the fulfillment of Malachi 3-4 and John's prophecy, it is there that Torah passed away, and not before.

Where ever you place the fulfillment of Malachi 3-4 and John's prophecy, the Law of Moses would (or will!) remain valid until that time.

Let me drive this point home a bit more. In Exodus 22 YHVH said that when Israel violated the law, He would punish them by the edge of the sword. This is a corporate, national judgment. Likewise, in Deuteronomy 27 the curses contained there are the introduction to what is called the Law of Blessings and Cursings (hereafter L-B-C) of chapter 28-30.

In a nutshell, the L-B-C delineated and defined the punishments that would come on the nation for violation of Torah, which it repeatedly called "the law" or "the book of the law" etc.. Some ten times those terms are utilized to speak of the Blessings and Cursings.

So, per Moses and Israel, the L-B-C was "the law." Notice just a couple of examples from Deuteronomy:

28:61 - "Also every sickness and every plague, which is not written in this Book of the Law, will the LORD bring upon you until you are destroyed.

29:21 - "And the LORD would separate him from all the tribes of Israel for adversity, according to all the curses of the covenant that are written in this Book of the Law,

30:10 - "if you obey the voice of the LORD your God, to keep His commandments and His statutes which are written in this Book of the Law, and if you turn to the LORD your God with all your heart and with all your soul.

31:26 - "Take this Book of the Law, and put it beside the ark of the covenant of the LORD your God, that it may be there as a witness against you;

Very clearly, Deuteronomy was called and considered to be "the law." It was also called "the covenant" and this is significant.

Now, read again Joshua 8:32-34:

"And there, in the presence of the children of Israel, he wrote on the stones a copy of the law of Moses, which he had written. Then all Israel, with their elders and officers and judges, stood on either side of the ark before the priests, the Levites, who bore the ark of the covenant of the LORD, the stranger as well as he who was born among them. Half of them were in front of Mount Gerazim and half of them in front of Mount Ebal, as Moses the servant of the LORD had commanded before, that they should bless the people of Israel. And afterward he read all the words of the law, the blessings and the cursings, according to all that is written in the Book of the Law."

Before analyzing this text a bit further than we did earlier, we need to see its background. In Deuteronomy 27, after Moses had given the law again, he then gave instructions to Joshua and Israel about what they were to do when they entered the promised land.

He instructed that when they crossed Jordan and entered the land that they were to erect some large stones, whitewash them and then, "You shall write on them all the words of this law" (v. 3).... you shall write very plainly on the stones all the words of this law" (v. 8).

So, Joshua and Israel were to erect large stones of testimony and inscribe on those stones "the law." What law was that?

It was the law they had received at Sinai being reiterated that day, Torah.

Now, we return to Joshua and we are told that Israel had now entered the land as promised. Joshua, in compliance with Moses' directions, there, in the presence of the children of Israel, "he wrote on the stones a copy of the law of Moses." Thus, the covenant / law given at Sinai, and reiterated at Horeb, was "the law of Moses."

But, notice also that after he had inscribed the law of Moses on those tablets, that he called on Israel, once again, to swear allegiance to "the law" under penalty of incurring the curses found in "the law."

Notice that it says: "Afterward he read all the words of the law, the blessings and the cursings, according to all that is written in the Book of the Law."

So, the L-B-C was "the law of Moses." It was "the book of the law." It was, simply, "the law." There is no way to deny that these terms were being used synonymously. Not only was the L-B-C "the law" but as we will see momentarily, the L-B-C was likewise prophecy. The implications of this are astounding, but, seldom explored. For the moment, let me make my point.

The L-B-C (Deuteronomy 28-30) was "the law of Moses", and "the law."

Not one single iota, not the tiniest of the minutia of "the law," "the law of Moses" could pass until it was all fulfilled (Matthew 5:17-18).

John, as Elijah, proclaimed the imminent fulfillment of the Law of Blessings and Curses at the Day of the Lord against Israel for her violation of Torah, in fulfillment of Malachi 3-4.

Therefore, until the fulfillment of John's prophecy of the Day of the Lord against Israel for violation of Torah, (in fulfillment of Malachi 3-4) "the law of Moses" (the Law of Blessings and Cursing) would remain valid.

Note also that since the Law of Blessings and Cursing (the "law of Moses) would remain valid until the Day of the Lord against Israel that John proclaimed, then *all of Torah, every jot and every tittle of "the law of Moses,"* remained (remains?) valid and binding. until the Day of the Lord against Israel that John proclaimed.

Remember, Jesus did not say that when *some* jots and some tittles are fulfilled that Torah would pass. He said that until every jot and every tittle was "fully accomplished" none of it would pass away.

There is another element here that is all but totally ignored or overlooked in the literature. That is that not only was the L-B-C "the law" it was likewise "the covenant."

Notice Deuteronomy 29:21: "And the LORD would separate him from all the tribes of Israel for adversity, according to all the curses of the covenant that are written in this Book of the Law." The implications of this are great, so let's take a closer look.

The L-B-C– the law of Moses-- was "the covenant" It was, in other words, *the Mosaic Covenant.* It is indefensible to dichotomize the Law of Moses into disparate elements, disjunctive aspects, unrelated tenets.

So, the L-B-C was "the law." It was "the law of Moses." It was "the Mosaic Covenant." This is just another way of saying that the Law of Moses was "the law" and "the law" was the Mosaic Covenant. *This is not just a semantic game.* This is an important concept that needs to be grasped and accepted.

The Law of Blessings and Cursings was "the law."
It was "the law of Moses."
It was "the Mosaic *Covenant.*"
This is just another way of saying that the Law of Moses was "the law" and "the law" was the Mosaic Covenant.
Do you catch the power of that?

And since Jesus said that not one single jot or tittle of "the law" would pass until it was all fulfilled, fully accomplished, then this means that until God had fulfilled every single aspect of *the Mosaic*

Covenant, the L-B-C, not the slightest part of Torah would pass away. In light of this, we need to take another brief look at the ministry of John.

As we have seen, as Elijah, John proclaimed the imminent Day of the Lord in the application of the L-B-C– i.e. the curses of the Covenant. This means, without any doubt, that *God's covenant with Israel* would remain valid– applicable– until and to the time of the Day of the Lord foretold by John.

So, we ask the question once again: When, after John, but before the cross when the Law of Moses was ostensibly nailed to the cross, did the Lord come in the application of the L-B-C? The answer is indisputable: The Lord did not come in the application of the Law of Moses' covenantal sanctions, after John but before the cross. However, take a look at two key passages, Zechariah 11:10f and Romans 11:25-27.

Zechariah 11:9f–

"Then I said, 'I will not feed you. Let what is dying die, and what is perishing perish. Let those that are left eat each other's flesh. And I took m y staff, Beauty, and cut it in two, that I might break the covenant which I had made with all the peoples. So it was broken on that day. Thus the poor of the flock, who were watching me, knew that it was the word of the LORD. Then I said to them, 'If it is agreeable to you, give me my wages; and if not, refrain.' So they weighed out for my wages thirty pieces of silver. Then I cut in two my other staff, Bonds, that I might break the brotherhood between Judah and Israel."

For brevity notice a couple of key points.

1.) God said that the time was coming in which He would no longer "feed" Israel. This terminology is highly significant, covenantally speaking. It means that the time was coming when God would no longer provide for Israel.

2.) That time would be when they would "eat each other's flesh." This is a direct referent to the L-B-C (Deuteronomy 28:48-57)! In other words, Zechariah, like Malachi, foretold the time when God would bring on Israel the Mosaic Covenant sanctions of wrath, for violating that covenant. And, we cannot miss the fact that Zechariah was predicting a corporate, nationalistic judgment just as Exodus 22 threatened.

Of course, anyone even remotely familiar with Josephus knows that he chronicles how in the siege of Jerusalem, which both ancient and modern historians and commentators acknowledge was foretold in Deuteronomy 28:48f, the inhabitants of Jerusalem did in fact eat the flesh of one another.

What is so significant about this is that while Jerusalem was attacked several times after Zechariah, *none* of those sieges approached the severity of AD 70. So far as I can determine, none were so severe that the inhabitants turned to cannibalism.

So, just like there was no Day of the Lord after John but before the cross in the application of Mosaic Covenant sanctions, there was likewise no siege of Jerusalem after Zechariah, but before the cross, in fulfillment of Mosaic Covenant sanctions.

3.) The time foretold by Zechariah is when God would "break the covenant which I had made with all the peoples." He would dissolve the covenantal brotherhood between Judah and Israel.[127]

4.) All of this would occur "in the day" when the Servant would be betrayed for thirty pieces of silver. Of course, there can be no doubt of the application of this prophecy.

So, Zechariah foretold the generation when God's Messiah would be betrayed. The application of the Mosaic Covenant sanctions and the ensuing dissolution of the covenant bond would be as a result of that betrayal. There is a direct cause and effect here.

---

[127] This prediction seems, on the surface, to contradict the prophecy of Ezekiel 37 and other prophecies that anticipated the "restoration" and "reunion" of the two houses. However, when one understands that God was going to destroy the Old Covenant bond, and create a New Covenant bond, radically different in nature (as Jeremiah 31 foretold) there is no actual conflict. Hebrews 8 makes it abundantly clear that Christ was fulfilling the promise of Ezekiel 37, and yet, Torah, the old "bond" between the two houses, was "ready to vanish."

This cause and effect concept brings the continuing validity of Torah into sharp focus. God was going to "no longer feed" Israel due to her rejection of her Messiah. He was going to bring a judgment on her so severe that they would turn to cannibalism, just as the L-B-C foretold. And, He would finally dissolve the covenantal bond between the two houses.

Now, if the cause and effect is admitted, then one can hardly argue that Torah, the covenant bond, and the ground for God's covenantal sanctions as described in Zechariah, was abolished at the cross. The cross, in the cause and effect framework, was the reason for the application of the Mosaic Covenant sanctions-- *40 years after the cross.*

Since it is, as we have noted, indisputably true that you cannot apply covenantal sanctions if the covenant and its sanctions are no longer valid, then the cause and effect principle in Zechariah 11 serves as *prima facie* proof that Torah did not pass at the cross. And if the L-B-C did not pass at the cross, then not one jot or one tittle of the Law of Moses passed at the cross. Let me put it like this:

Zechariah 11:9-12 foretold the time when God would bring to bear the Mosaic Covenant sanctions of wrath (the L-B-C) on Israel.

Those sanctions would be applied due to Israel's guilt of violating Torah, i.e. her rejection and killing of her own Messiah.[128]

Thus, as a result of killing Jesus, God would bring the Mosaic Covenant sanctions (the L-B-C) on Israel.

That time when be when they would eat one another's flesh– AD 70.

---

[128] According to Peter in Acts 3:19ff, obedience to Jesus equated to obedience to Moses, i.e. Torah. Rejection of Jesus would result in being, "utterly cut off out from among (*ek tou laou) the* people" (Acts 3:23). This is Zechariah recapitulated.

God brought to bear the Mosaic Covenant sanctions (the L-B-C) on Israel in AD 70.

Therefore, the Mosaic Covenant sanctions (the L-B-C) were still valid in AD 70.

Without any doubt, the Mosaic Covenant remained valid until AD 70. Interestingly, some commentators agree with this, although they do not see the implications for their own theology. Notice what Thomas Ice says about Luke 21:22 and Jesus' prediction of the impending vengeance and wrath that came in AD 70.   "Those first century days are called the 'days of vengeance for Jerusalem is under the divine judgment of covenantal sanctions recorded in Leviticus 26 and Deuteronomy 28. Luke notes that God's vengeance on His elect nation 'is in order that all things that are written may be fulfilled.' Jesus is telling the nation that God will fulfill all the curses of the Mosaic Covenant because of Israel's disobedience. He will not relent and merely bring to pass a partial fulfillment of His vengeance. Some of the passages that Jesus says will be fulfilled include the following: Leviticus 26:27-33; Deuteronomy 28:49-63; Deuteronomy 32: 19-27; 1 Kings 9:1-9; Jeremiah 6:1-6; 26:1-9; Daniel 9:26; Hosea 8:1-10:15; Micah 3:12; Zechariah 11:6."[129]

Notice that Ice posits AD 70 as the fulfillment of the L-B-C, i.e. Deuteronomy 28:49-63. And yet, Ice nonetheless claims, "The sacrifices of the millennium will not be a return to the Mosaic Law,[130]

---

[129] Thomas Ice, *The Great Tribulation Past or Future?* A formal written debate between Thomas Ice and Kenneth Gentry, *(Grand Rapids, Kregel, 1999)*98.

[130] Ice's rampant confusion and self-contradiction is then on display when he argues concerning the Tribulation temple (which is not the millennial temple in the dispensational paradigm): "During three and a half years of peace, Judaism is revived, and traditional sacrifices and ceremonies are re-instituted in the rebuilt temple in Jerusalem." (*Prophecy Watch*, 60). Now, if the revival of Judaism and re-institution of "traditional sacrifices" is not the restoration of the Mosaic Law, what is it? The traditional

since the Law has forever been fulfilled and discontinued through Christ (Romans 6:1, 15; 7:1-6; 1 Corinthians 9:20,21; 2 Corinthians 3:7-11; Galatians 4:1-7; 5:18; Hebrews 8:13; 10:1-14)."[131]

Then, amazingly, he exhibits confusion even on the sacrificial system that he claims Christ removed, when he says of the millennial temple and the sacrificial cultus, "In the millennial temple, all that was prescribed and initiated in the Old Testament ceremonial and ritual activities will come to completion and their fullest meaning." (*Prophecy*, 256).

So, per Ice, the Law of Moses was completely fulfilled and removed by Christ in the first century. However, it was not completely fulfilled until AD 70 when total fulfillment took place. However, he then posits the total fulfillment of the Law of Moses sacrificial cultus in the millennial temple.

To say that this is a confused theology is an understatement. Very clearly, if the typological sacrifices of the Law of Moses do not come to their final fulfillment until the millennial temple is built, then not one jot or one tittle of the Law of Moses will pass until that millennial temple is built.

Remember, Torah and its sacrifices were, "shadows of good things to come" and would remain valid until what they foreshadowed came to full accomplishment (Colossians 2:14-16; Hebrews 9:6f; 10:1-3). You cannot have Torah removed at the cross, then fulfilled in AD 70, and yet, still awaiting the final realization of the shadows of Torah in a yet future millennial temple, without thereby logically demanding that the Law of Moses remains valid until that proposed millennium. If the law passed, then it passed. If any of it awaits final fulfillment, in any way whatsoever, then none of it passed.

---

sacrifices of Judaism were taken directly from the Law of Moses. Thus, the re-institution of traditional sacrifices is, *prima facie*, the restoration of the Mosaic Law.

[131] Thomas Ice and Timothy Demy, *Prophecy Watch*, (Eugene, Or. Harvest House, 1998)258.

You cannot have Torah annulled at the cross, then, somehow fulfilled in AD 70, and then, still awaiting the final realization of the shadows of Torah in a yet future millennial temple, without thereby logically demanding that the Law of Moses remains valid until that proposed millennium.

If it passed, it passed.

If it was not all fully accomplished, then none of it passed.

The confusion and contradiction of the millennial view of Torah is serious. But, in reality, that confusion is no worse than any of the other theologies and eschatologies.

Remember that both the amillennial and postmillennial eschatologies posit the removal of the sacrificial cultus at the cross. In other words, they tell us that *part* of the Law of Moses was removed while part of it, i.e. the prophetic element, remains valid. As we shall see below, this is completely untenable.

For now, it is critical to see once again the relationship between the L-B-C, *as God's covenant with Israel*, and the fulfillment of John the Baptizer's ministry. It is difficult to over-emphasize that connection.

John, as Elijah, proclaimed the impending Great and Terrible Day of the Lord, against Israel, for the violation of Torah (Malachi 3:5; 4:4-6).

That Day of the Lord would be the application of Mosaic Covenant Wrath, i.e. the L-B-C.

Therefore, where ever you posit the fulfillment of John's prediction of "the wrath about to come," the full application of the "axe at the root" and "the winnowing fork" that was already in Christ's hand, it is there and to that time that God's covenant with Israel would remain valid and binding.

Since it is indisputably true that Christ did not come in judgment of Israel, in the application of the L-B-C, after John, but before the cross, then, to repeat our argument, it is irrefutably true that the God did not leave Israel and Torah behind at the cross.

In light of Zechariah's prophecy of when that Mosaic Covenant L-B-C would be both applied and terminated, i.e. when both houses of

91

Israel ate each other's flesh, this adds additional support to the fact that AD 70 was the time when the Mosaic Covenant provisions of Blessings and Cursings was both applied and terminated. That is when God left Israel and Torah behind, and not before.

Let's take a look at another text that demonstrates that God's covenant with Israel was not left behind at the cross.

Romans 11:25-27 –

"For I do not desire, brethren, that you should be ignorant of this mystery, lest you should be wise in your own opinion, that blindness in part has happened to Israel until the fullness of the Gentiles has come in. 26 And so all Israel will be saved, as it is written:

"The Deliverer will come out of Zion, And He will turn away ungodliness from Jacob; For this is My covenant with them, When I take away their sins."

Notice that YHVH's promise that the Savior would come out of Zion to take away Israel's sin was *a covenantal promise.* Clearly then, God's covenant with Israel would remain in effect until He brought His promises to Israel to their climax and consummation.

This can be viewed in two different, but merging ways.

First, the Old Covenant itself promised that the time was coming when God would offer salvation to His people (Isaiah 46:13; 49:6f, etc.) and then to the nations. So, the promise of salvation was itself a covenantal promise.

Second, the means by which God would take away Israel's sin was to be through the New Covenant. In contrast to the Old Covenant that could never take away sin (Hebrews 10:1-4) God promised to make a new, different covenant, "and their sins and iniquities will I remember no more" (Jeremiah 31:29-31).

So, in essence, the Old Covenant promise of salvation would be fulfilled when the promised New Covenant would be fully accomplished.[132] But, there is more here than even this.

---

[132] Compare for instance Hebrews 9:15f and Hebrews 10:10f where the New Covenant is posited as the means of salvation and the consummation of Christ's sitting at the right hand of the Father, awaiting final victory. The connection

92

Notice that Paul draws on two Old Covenant prophecies of the salvation of Israel, Isaiah 27 and Isaiah 59. I will be brief but I want to notice some particularly relevant elements from each of these texts that related directly to our discussion of the L-B-C above.

Both contexts of Isaiah 27 and 59 accused Israel of violating Torah, and specifically of being guilty of shedding innocent blood (Isaiah 26:21; 59:3-7). In Isaiah 24:5 Israel was accused specifically of "breaking the everlasting covenant" and as a result, the "city of confusion" (v. 10) that sat "in the midst of the land" (v. 13) was doomed to destruction. Here is the threat of covenantal sanctions for violation of Torah. This is the L-B-C-- the Law of Moses-- being applied.

And yet, while YHVH would bring a desolating destruction on the city and temple (25:1-5) He would also establish the Messianic Banquet and destroy death in the day of Israel's salvation (25:6-10). He would avenge the shed blood of the saints (26:21), destroy Leviathan the enemy, and gather the dead from the four winds with the sounding of the Great Trumpet, the Trumpet of the Great Jubilee (27:13).

It is in verses 9-10 of chapter 27 that God promised to take away Israel's sin. But, paradoxically, He would take away her sin by bringing that destruction on her, in the day that He made the altar like chalkstone. In that day He would forget the rebellious people and bring desolation on them.[133]

Notice that in Isaiah 59 God accused Israel of shedding innocent blood and being a people quick to violence, three times. This three-fold accusation drives home the seriousness of the accusation. As a result of their sin God would put on the garments of vengeance and come in judgment of the guilty. At the same time, He would come in salvation of the righteous remnant. And all of this, once again, would be in fulfillment of His covenant with Israel: "this is my covenant with them" (v. 21). So, in fulfillment of the L-B-C, YHVH would come

---

between the New Covenant and final victory / salvation is clear.

[133] This is the doctrine of Blood Atonement at work. Those guilty of shedding innocent blood (26:21) would perish. The righteous remnant would be spared.

exacting vengeance on Israel for shedding innocent blood. But, He would also bring salvation for the remnant.

So, what we have are the elements of both judgment and salvation in the same context. We cannot create a false contradiction here and say, as millennialists are prone to do, "Well, it can't be the time of Israel's salvation because it says He would destroy the rebellious people." The fact is that Israel would be saved through judgment, not saved *from* judgment. The majority would perish, the righteous remnant would be purified and delivered. Salvation and destruction go hand in hand.

Of course, what cannot go un-noticed is the fact that in Romans 11:26-27 Paul cites both Isaiah 27 and Isaiah 59 as he anticipates the salvation of Israel: "And so, all Israel shall be saved, 'The Deliverer will come out of Zion and He will turn away ungodliness from Jacob For this is my covenant with them, when I take away their sin.'"

Let me state my argument here as succinctly as possible.

The coming of the Lord of Romans 11:26-27 is the coming of the Lord foretold in Isaiah 27 and Isaiah 59.

The coming of the Lord in Isaiah 27 and Isaiah 59 would be in application of the L-B-C sanctions of the Law of Blood Atonement (the Mosaic Covenant), i.e. judgment for shedding innocent blood.

Therefore, the coming of the Lord in Romans 11:26-27 would be in application of the L-B-C sanctions of the Law of Blood Atonement (the Mosaic Covenant), i.e. judgment for shedding innocent blood.

It is astounding to me that this aspect of Romans 11 is so grossly overlooked. Focus is generally on the question of whether God will one day save "all Israel." However, as I have read the literature it is quite remarkable that I have yet to find a commentator who comments on Paul's use of Isaiah 27 and 59, other than to simply note that he does in fact cite those prophecies.

None of the commentators examined spend any time examining the significance of those prophecies and how they might aid our understanding of Romans 11. *How can we say that we have done a*

94

solid exegesis of Romans 11 if we ignore the prophetic source of Paul's hope?

In the postmillennial world, Romans 11 has historically been the foundation for the doctrine of the salvation of the majority of ethnic Israel at the end of the Christian age.

Bahnsen chronicles this in his *Victory in Jesus* book.[134] In fact, Bahnsen says, "The Westminster divines looked forward to the overthrow of the Roman Antichrist, the expansion of the true church by the conversion of the Jews and the fulness of the Gentiles, and an age of blessing upon the church through the rule of Christ." (1999, p. 89).[135] It is not to much to say that in historical and creedal Postmillennialism, Romans 11 is a foundational eschatological text.

We should take note, however that a significant, we might even say *incredible*, thing is happening in the postmillennial camp. As Bahnsen notes, historically, Romans 11:25-27 has been a foundational text to support the idea that at the end of the Christian age "all Israel" i.e. the

---

[134] Greg L. Bahnsen, *Victory In Jesus, The Bright Hope of Postmillennialism,* (Texarkana, Ar., Covenant Media Press, 1999, Bahnsen Trust)83++.

[135] There is another irony here. Postmillennialists condemn full preterists such as myself because we violate the creeds. Yet, it can easily be shown that many of the most prominent postmillennialists of the day, Gentry, DeMar, Seriah, Mathison, McDurmon, etc. openly reject the foundational eschatology of the creeds as iterated by Bahnsen, i.e that Christ's second coming would be to destroy the Roman Catholic Pope! Similarly, these same "reformers" take positions on many, many key eschatological texts which positions are not to be found in the creeds. It is fair to ask: if these "reformers" can reject the creedal eschatology regarding the Catholic Church, and take almost unprecedented (non-creedal) positions on foundational eschatological texts, why can't they go ahead and reject the futurism of the creeds, like true preterists?

majority of ethnic Jews, will be converted to Christ. Kenneth Gentry continues to affirm that traditional postmillennial view.[136]

However, lately, James Jordan has said that Romans 11 was fulfilled in AD 70.[137] Gary DeMar also now takes the view that Paul was speaking of the events of AD 70.[138] Joel McDurmon seems also to espouse the AD 70 fulfillment. Jonathan Seriah says Romans 11:26f looks back at the cross. So, within the postmillennial camp there are now three radically different positions on Romans 11.[139]

Amillennialists likewise struggle with Romans 11. It is commonly held however, that Paul was not predicting a coming of the Lord that was future to him. Riddlebarger expresses a commonly held amillennial view: "Paul, therefore, probably understands the future tenses of the Isaiah prophecy as fulfilled in the first coming of Christ, which set in motion the apostolic mission of the church."[140] Riddlebarger, while noting that Paul cites Isaiah 27, 59 gives not one word of commentary on the significance of that prophetic source. He says *nothing* about the actual content and context of Isaiah 59.

Notice the unmistakable covenant context of the prophecy of Isaiah 59. In verse 10 the people speak of being like blind men groping for the wall in mid-day. This is a direct allusion to Deuteronomy 28:29, where God said that when Israel would forsake Torah, He would strike them

---

[136] Kenneth Gentry, (*Thine is the Kingdom*, (Vallecito, CA., Chalcedon 2003)13ff, 169).

[137] James B. Jordan, "The Future of Israel Re-examined," Biblical Horizons, No. 27 July, 1991.

[138] Jonathin Seriah *(The End of All Things,* Moscow, ID, Canon Press, 1999)109.

[139] To say that the postmillennial "division" on Romans 11 is ironic is a huge understatement. Kenneth Gentry and other postmillennialists have refused to formally debate preterists because they claim preterists are divided and do not even agree among themselves. And yet, now, in regard to what has historically been a foundational eschatological text among postmillennialists, there is growing disagreement!

[140] Kim Riddlebarger, *A Case for Amillennialism: Understanding the End Times*, (Grand Rapids, Baker, 2003).

and they would be like blind men groping for the wall. And remember, it was that sinful situation that would call forth the coming of the Lord in Isaiah 59:7f, His coming in judgment. Thus, once again, the context of the parousia in Isaiah– and thus, Romans 11– is the application of Mosaic Covenant sanctions.

In two formal written debates, my opponents have vacillated wildly on Paul's use of Isaiah. In my debate with (preterist) Kurt Simmons he initially claimed that Isaiah 27 and 59 were not Messianic, *at all*. Likewise, in my debate with amillennialist Jerry McDonald, he also initially claimed that neither Isaiah 27 or 59 were Messianic.

I noted in response to these claims that if this were true it meant that Paul was citing two prophecies that had nothing whatsoever to do with what he was discussing. I challenged each of these men to give the hermeneutic that would explain why Paul, in discussing his hope for the salvation of Israel would quote two prophecies that had nothing– *absolutely nothing* per their claims– to do with his hope and his discussion?

Simmons and McDonald both changed their position repeatedly during our discussions, vacillating between the non-Messianic application of Isaiah, a typological application of the prophecies, claiming the prophecies were fulfilled at the cross, or resorting to simply ignoring my discussion of the texts.[141] Such is the confusion that exists in the amillennial world in regard to Romans 11.[142]

---

[141] My debate with Simmons is now in book form: *The End of Torah, at the Cross or AD 70?*, available from both my websites, Amazon, and other retailers. The debate with McDonald is on both of my websites.

[142] A quick anecdote here. In 1982 I was preparing for my first formal public debate, with a premillennialist. I knew my opponent normally relied on Romans 11:25f, so, I went to lunch with a friend of mine, a prominent professor at a Bible college. I asked for help with Romans 11. He looked at me for a moment and then said, to paraphrase, "Don, let's just hope your opponent does not go to Romans 11 and camp out. I can't help you with that text. It is just a mystery to me." As a fifth generation member of the amillennial world, before becoming a preterist, I can well testify to the confusion in that world concerning Romans 11.

Dispensationalists claim that Romans 11 as one of their key supportive texts for a yet future salvation of Israel, which they posit during the seven year tribulation period, when, under extreme duress from the Antichrist, Israel finally calls out to Jesus as their Messiah, and he comes and saves them.

The problem for the dispensationalist is that although they cite Romans 11, like the amillennial and postmillennial commentators, they ignore what Isaiah 27 and 59 predicted. In fact, the dispensational view has no place in it for what Isaiah foretold, the coming of the Lord in judgment of Israel for shedding innocent blood.

Dispensationalism holds that it is Old Covenant Israel that is persecuted by the anti-Christ. She is the "innocent victim" under his bloody hand. But, they cry out to YHVH, finally in faith in Christ, and he comes on the clouds and destroys the anti-Christ.

There is nothing in the millennial schema that matches the prophecy of Isaiah 27 or 59. They do not acknowledge that it is Israel–not some Man of Sin-- that is guilty of shedding innocent blood. They do not acknowledge that the coming of Christ in view is against Israel, i.e. against the nation, for shedding that innocent blood. They claim that the nation is delivered from judgment, when both prophecies affirm the destruction of the nation at Christ's coming.

We are thus once again confronted with a hermeneutical problem. If Paul was predicting a yet future deliverance of the nation of Israel, from the bloody persecution at the hands of the Man of Sin, why in the name of reason does he quote from prophecies that do not mention a Man of Sin? Isaiah accuses *Israel*, not a foreign anti-Christ, of being the persecutor of the saints. Isaiah foretold destruction of the nation (27:9f) not deliverance. He only offered deliverance for the righteous remnant.

So, just as amillennialists and postmillennialists ignore the actual prophetic source of Romans 11, the dispensationalists are equally guilty of eisegesis.

What is missing in all three futurist paradigms is the indisputable fact that neither Isaiah 27 or 59 mentions the cross, and the context is clearly not the cross. This naturally raises a serious challenge to the posit by Riddlebarger that Paul was utilizing Isaiah to look back at the cross. There were many OT prophecies of the cross, and yet, Paul did not cite any of them. Instead, he cited two prophecies that are very specific predictions of the coming of the Lord in application of Mosaic Covenant sanctions against Israel for shedding innocent blood! In light of Matthew 23 that was patently not fulfilled at the cross.

Why in the name of reason would Paul cite two prophecies of the coming of the Lord in judgment on Israel for shedding innocent blood, if he had the cross in mind? What is the hermeneutical justification for such a claim?

Why in the name of reason would Paul cite two prophecies of the coming of the Lord in judgment on Israel for shedding innocent blood, if he had the _cross_ in mind? What is the hermeneutical justification for such a claim?

What is missing in all three futurist views and applications of Romans 11 is that their views conflict with their claims about the end of the Law of Moses. Remember, all three futurist views claim, to varying degrees, that the Law of Moses was removed at the cross. But, if the Law of Moses, the L-B-C, was annulled at the cross, how could Paul be anticipating the fulfillment of Isaiah 27 and 59 which were prophecies of the application of the L-B-C? Do you see the problem? It is insurmountable.

Here then is the problem stated:

The coming of the Lord in Romans 11:26-27 would be in fulfillment of Isaiah 27 and 59.

The coming of the Lord in Isaiah 27 and Isaiah 59 would be in application of the L-B-C sanctions of the Law of Blood Atonement (the Mosaic Covenant), i.e. judgment for shedding innocent blood.

Therefore the coming of the Lord in Romans 11:26-27 would be in application of the L-B-C sanctions of the Law of Blood Atonement (the Mosaic Covenant), i.e. judgment for shedding innocent blood.

Now, what this demands, *prima facie*, is that the Law of Moses, the Mosaic Covenant, the L-B-C, would remain valid, binding and in effect until the coming of the Lord in application of the L-B-C sanctions of the Law of Blood Atonement (the Mosaic Covenant), i.e. in judgment of Israel for shedding innocent blood. When did that take place? Jesus answers that question definitively in Matthew 23:29-37:

> "Woe to you, scribes and Pharisees, hypocrites! Because you build the tombs of the prophets and adorn the monuments of the righteous, and say, 'If we had lived in the days of our fathers, we would not have been partakers with them in the blood of the prophets.' "Therefore you are witnesses against yourselves that you are sons of those who murdered the prophets. Fill up, then, the measure of your fathers' guilt. Serpents, brood of vipers! How can you escape the condemnation of hell? Therefore, indeed, I send you prophets, wise men, and scribes: some of them you will kill and crucify, and some of them you will scourge in your synagogues and persecute from city to city, that on you may come all the righteous blood shed on the earth, from the blood of righteous Abel to the blood of Zechariah, son of Berechiah, whom you murdered between the temple and the altar. Assuredly, I say to you, all these things will come upon this generation. O Jerusalem, Jerusalem, the one who kills the prophets and stones those who are sent to her! How often I wanted to gather your children together, as a hen gathers her chicks under her wings, but you were not willing!"

Words could hardly be clearer or more emphatic. Here is Jesus' prediction of the coming application of the Law of Blood Atonement, the L-B-C, the Law of Moses. That judgment of Israel for shedding the blood of all the righteous was to be in the first century judgment of Jerusalem. Paul agrees with Jesus about that coming judgment.

In Acts 13, Paul preached to the Jews in the synagogue in Antioch. The Jews rejected that message however, so, here is what Paul said: "Beware therefore, lest what has been spoken in the prophets come upon you: 'Behold, you despisers, Marvel and perish! For I work a work in your days, A work which you will by no means believe, Though one were to declare it to you.'" (Acts 13:40f).

Paul is citing Habakkuk 1:5 where the prophet foretold the impending destruction of Jerusalem at the hands of the Chaldeans. Why was God going to bring the Babylonians against His people? Because they had violated Torah, and were now subject to the sanctions in the L-B-C. They had shed innocent blood (Jeremiah 2, 7). They had oppressed the foreigners Exodus 22:21-24; Deuteronomy 27:19f). They had mistreated the widows and the orphans (Jeremiah 7. Remember Malachi 3:5?). As a result, the Day of the Lord came against them (Jeremiah 4:24f; Zephaniah 1-2, etc.). This was the application of the Law of Blood Atonement. It was the L-B-C. It was the Law of Moses, the Mosaic *Covenant* sanctions, being applied.

And now, in Acts 13 Paul was threatening his audience with that very kind of thing, "Beware let that which is written in the prophets come on you."

It is somewhat astounding that many commentators fail to see Paul's warnings as the threat of covenant sanctions.

In my written debate with Jerry McDonald, I took note of Acts 13 and its covenantal source and framework. McDonald simply denied that connection, (but gave no scriptural support) with his oft-repeated claim that the Torah passed at the cross, therefore, Paul could not be threatening Israel with covenant sanctions. His presuppositional, *a priori*, circular reasoning and theology was painfully evident.

The indisputable fact is that the Babylonian invasion was the application of Mosaic Covenant sanctions as a result of Israel's violation of Torah. And now, Paul threatened his Jewish audience, with that kind of judgment: "Beware let that which is written in the prophets come on you."

It is unthinkable to suggest that Paul or the Jews would think of his warnings divorced from covenant sanctions. As we have noted above, Israel well understood that God had came against them in the past.

Elliott shows that the siege of Jerusalem in BC 63 by Ptolemy was considered a covenantal curse by Israel. He cites the Psalms of Solomon 17-19, that cites Deuteronomy 11:16-17 for what had happened: "Take heed lest... he shut up the heavens. so that there be no rain.' or 1 Kings 8:35– "When heaven is shut up and there is no rain because they have sinned against thee." Elliott goes ahead to say that there is clear evidence that in Israel there was the understanding that

101

covenantal violation would bring cosmic implications– i.e. no rain, no crops, cattle dying, etc.[143]

So, the Assyrian captivity and the Babylonian invasion (as well as other national catastrophes) were understood by Israel to be a direct result of her violation of Torah, and the application of Mosaic Covenant sanctions of corporate punishment. And now, in Acts 13 Paul warned the Jews of his day that they must obey his word, or suffer the same fate as their forefathers. And yet, we are told, that what Paul was threatening was totally unrelated to what had happened to their predecessors, totally disconnected from covenant sanctions. It is difficult to imagine a more illogical suggestion.

That means that what Paul was threatening in Acts 13 is what Jesus foretold in Matthew 24:15f and this is nothing less than the threat of Covenant judgment against Israel. This is confirmed by his prediction of the coming Abomination of Desolation.

Jesus foretold the coming of the Great Tribulation– on Israel– as a result of the Abomination of Desolation (Matthew 24:15-21). The Tribulation is what Paul had in mind in Acts 13. As Pitre has noted, the Abomination of Desolation must be viewed as a desolation, *a covenant violation*, so bad that it would lead to the desolation of the Temple. Likewise, Grey comments on Jesus' terminology of the Abomination of Desolation: "'Desolating sacrilege' literally means 'the sacrilege that causes desolation.' It causes desolation." It cause desolation because the profanation of the temple incurs God's judgment which ultimately leads to the destruction of the temple."[144]

In Israel's history, the profanation of the Temple through sinful actions– actions in violation of Torah– led directly to desolation:

"The adversary has spread his hand Over all her pleasant things; For she has seen the nations enter her sanctuary, Those whom You commanded Not to enter Your assembly".... "The Lord has spurned His altar, He has abandoned His sanctuary; He has given up the walls of her palaces Into the hand of the enemy. They have made a noise in the house of the LORD As on the day of a set feast.

---

[143] Mark Adam Elliott, *The Survivors of Israel*, (Grand Rapids, Eerdmans, 2000)284.

[144] Timothy Gray, *The Temple In The Gospel of Mark*, (Grand Rapids, Baker Academic, 2008)141.

(Lamentations 1:10; 2:7). So, violation of Torah would (and had) lead directly to desolation of the temple.[145] (Lamentations 1:10; 2:7).[146]

So, throughout history, judgments on Israel / Jerusalem were always a direct result of her violation of Torah. Abominable acts led to tribulation. I suggest that all of this demands that the Abomination of Desolation and ensuing Tribulation must be seen as a covenantal curse. If the Abomination of Desolation demands that Israel's sin would lead to desolation, then it would be Israel's violation of Torah and desecration of the temple that would lead to its Desolation. And of course, directly connected to this is the rejection of Jesus and his Word

---

[145] It is important to note that in Isaiah's prediction of the Messianic Banquet and the resurrection, he says it would be in the day when the city and temple would be turned over to foreigners (25:1-2). God would abandon the people He had created and turn the altar of the temple into chalkstone (27:10-12). Just as God had brought covenantal sanctions on Israel and Judah in the past, turning the city and temple over to foreigners, He would do the same *in the day of the resurrection!* So, once again, the framework of eschatology is firmly established as "Covenant Eschatology" not historical eschatology. It is posited as the time of judgment on Israel, not the passing of the material cosmos, or the end of the Christian age.

[146] For an extensive, and to my knowledge unprecedented, discussion of the direct relationship between Lamentations and the book of Revelation, see my *Who Is This Babylon?* The language of Revelation is drawn directly from Jeremiah's lament over the fall of Jerusalem in BC 586 at the hands of the Chaldeans. That judgment came as a direct result of Israel's violation of Torah. John utilizes Jeremiah's language in anticipation of the imminent fall of "Babylon." The language is covenantal to the core, and all but demands that Revelation predicted the final downfall of Old Covenant Jerusalem.

and his disciples (Matthew 23:29-37)[147]– *the sin of shedding innocent blood.*[148]

Now, if God had left Israel and Torah behind at the cross, as is commonly claimed, then nothing that the Jews might do in the temple could be considered an Abomination. After all, from the perspective of those who say the Mosaic Covenant passed at the cross, that Jerusalem temple was now– post cross– just another building, with no covenantal significance, no covenantal standing. But, if that is true, *then how could there be an Abomination– a sinful desecration– in the temple?* How could the temple be defiled, if the temple had no standing, no validity, no covenant significance? You cannot defile that which is not defilable, and if the temple no longer had covenant standing after the cross, then it was no longer defilable.

So, all of this once again raises a serious obstacle to the view of Torah that is held by all futurist paradigms.

All futurist eschatologies posit the end of Torah, the L-B-C, which would include the Law of Blood Atonement, at the cross. And yet, here was Jesus, and Paul, predicting the yet future application of the L-B-C, the application of Mosaic Covenant sanctions.

How could Jesus be anticipating the fulfillment of the Mosaic Covenant sanctions if he knew that the Law of Moses was to be done away with at his cross? It is the epitome of illogic to suggest that Jesus was predicting the application of the L-B-C 40 years after he would invalidate, annul and remove those sanctions.

Notice the perfect harmony between Romans 11 and Matthew 23. Isaiah predicted the coming of the Lord in application of the L-B-C (and don't forget Zechariah 11) at the coming of the Lord in judgment of Israel for shedding innocent blood. Jesus predicted the coming judgment of Israel for shedding innocent blood, and that would occur at his parousia (Matthew 23-24:34).

---

[147] Don't forget that for Peter, rejection of Jesus was itself rejection of Moses and Torah (Acts 3).

[148] This of course brings us back full circle to Isaiah 27 and 59 (and other prophecies that could be given) which foretold the last days judgment of Israel for shedding innocent blood.

104

Paul, in Romans 11:26f, was living just a few short years before Jesus came in judgment of Israel for shedding innocent blood. He cites the two prophecies from Isaiah about the coming of the Lord in judgment of Israel for shedding innocent blood. And yet, we are supposed to believe that Paul did not have in mind the very thing that Isaiah foretold. He had in mind something totally unrelated, totally disconnected from what Isaiah foretold. What kind of convoluted hermeneutic, what kind of "exegesis" is this? To be blunt, this is nothing short of eisegesis, and preconceived ideology, not sound hermeneutic, not exegesis at all. It is fundamentally flawed. But now, let's bring John the Baptizer back into the discussion.

Remember that John, as Elijah, was to proclaim the coming of the Great and Terrible Day of the Lord, in the application of Mosaic Covenant sanctions, i.e. the L-B-C (Malachi 3:5.). As we have shown, John anticipated that Great Day as an imminent event; not something for his far distant future.

Also, we have demonstrated that from John until the cross, when Torah was supposedly invalidated and abrogated, there was no Day of the Lord against Israel. So, at the risk of sounding repetitious, this leaves us with few options:

➤ The prophecy of Malachi (and John) failed. The prophecies were not, and will not be fulfilled, thus falsifying Malachi, John and scripture as inspired prophecy / scripture.

➤ The prophecy of Malachi (and John) was fulfilled at some point after John and after the cross.

➤The prophecy of Malachi (and John) is yet to be fulfilled.

Option #1 is unacceptable and not even plausible, if we are willing to accept the testimony of history, and scripture. The point of fact is that Israel was judged, in the way described by Zechariah 11 and Malachi, and in harmony with how she had been judged in the past, i.e. through national judgment at the hands of invading armies.

Option #2 as just suggested, is the most viable option. However, if one accepts the fact that the judgment of Malachi and John occurred after the cross, then this is an open admission that the L-B-C remained valid until that time, i.e. AD 70.

Option #3 There are those who suggest that the prophecy of Malachi, and thus John, has not yet been fulfilled, but will be fulfilled

105

at the end of human history.[149] However, if that is the case, then clearly, Torah– all of it– remains valid.

Of course, those who posit the yet future fulfillment of Malachi (and John) also claim that the Law of Moses has been annulled. This is a self contradictory position. The imposition and application of the L-B-C is inseparably connected to the Day of the Lord of Malachi and John. That anticipated Day was to be God bringing to bear those Mosaic Covenant provisions for disobedience to Torah. So, once again, wherever one places their proposed fulfillment of the Day of the Lord foretold by Malachi and John, it is there that the Law remained valid, binding and applicable.

With this in mind, remember that both Isaiah 27 and 59 foretold the application of the Law of Blood Atonement, and the L-B-C, at the coming of the Lord in judgment of Israel for shedding innocent blood. That is the coming of the Lord Paul had in mind in Romans 11:26-27.

For those who, like Riddlebarger, claim that Paul was looking back at the cross, we ask again: why would Paul cite two prophecies of the coming of the Lord in judgment of Israel for shedding innocent blood, if he actually had the cross in mind?

The cross was in no way a judgment of Israel for shedding innocent blood. It was in fact, the basis for the judgment of Israel for killing him. It is wrong to even attempt to make the killing of Jesus to be the judgment of Israel for killing him! Those are two disparate actions. One is action, the other is reaction. One is action, the other is consequence for action.

Once we accept the fact that Paul's citation of Isaiah demands that he was anticipating the coming of the Lord in judgment of Israel for shedding innocent blood, this brings the entire issue of the passing of Torah sharply into focus. It means that until the coming of the Lord in fulfillment of Isaiah 27 and 59, God's covenant with Israel, including the sanctions for wrath, would remain valid.

---

[149] For instance, Greg Beale and D. A. Carson, in their massive, and helpful, *Commentary on the New Testament Use of the Old Testament,* (Grand Rapids, Baker Academic, Apollos,2007)1106. Beale and Carson list Malachi 3-4 as predictive of the end of history.

Furthermore, when we accept Jesus' word that his coming in vengeance and wrath on Jerusalem– for shedding innocent blood– was to be in that generation, then we have a prima facie argument for the continuance of the L-B-C, the Law of Blood Atonement, until AD 70.

There is no way to divorce Jesus' prediction of the impending judgment of Jerusalem for shedding innocent blood from a context of covenant curses. Historically, the Jews knew that God had judged them for shedding innocent blood (Jeremiah 2, 7, etc.). And that was *always* based on Torah, the Law of Blood Atonement, and the application of the covenant curses of Deuteronomy 28-32 and Leviticus 26.

It needs to be kept firmly in mind that *the gospel of Christ contains no covenantal sanctions such as the Law of Blood Atonement.* Thus, it will not do to argue that Torah passed, but that Jerusalem fell in fulfillment of New Covenant sanctions. The gospel is simply not a covenant that is geo-politically-nationalistically oriented.

Contrary to the Re-constructionist Movement that insists that Torah remains God's law– (well, at least *some* of Torah, for they say the ceremonial, sacrificial, cultus has passed[150])- the Law of Moses, all of it, was nigh unto passing, and did pass in AD 70.

The gospel did not replace the Law of Moses as a nationalistic constitution. It truly is a spiritual law, intended to govern a spiritual kingdom that is "not made with hands." So, to reiterate, the gospel has no provisions for nationalistic invasion and destruction such as that which occurred in the AD 70 judgment of Israel. That judgment was a covenantal judgment on Israel for violating the law of Moses. And of course, that means that Torah remain valid until that time.

So, what have we seen in this section? We have shown that the Law of Moses, "the law," included the L-B-C, and the Law of Blood Atonement. The inspired writers used the term "the law" and "the law of Moses" etc., interchangeably to refer to the L-B-C as "the law," "the covenant," "the law of Moses." It is therefore, a violation of the

---

[150] McDurmon for instance, says, "The epistle to the Hebrews teaches that all those Old covenant priestly ordinances are done away with" (McDurmon J -v- J, P. 90). He says on page 47 that in AD 70, "the symbol and ceremonies of that Old System– the Temple and sacrifices– were completely destroyed."

Biblical vernacular to suggest that in Matthew 5:17-18 Jesus had to have been speaking of a highly restricted, extremely limited aspect of the Law of Moses. There is no basis whatsoever for the claim that in Matthew 5, Jesus had only the sacrifices in mind; the sacrificial cultus had not even been mentioned.

So, we have established that the Law of Blessings and Cursings was "the law" and thus included in Jesus' statement that all of the law had to be fulfilled. We have likewise demonstrated that the L-B-C was "the covenant" and this means that until the L-B-C was fulfilled, that God's covenant with Israel would remain firm.

The Law Was Prophetic
The Prophets Foretold the Application
of Mosaic Covenant Sanctions

There is a third aspect to the L-B-C, (not to mention the Law of Blood Atonement) and that is the indisputable fact that it was *prophetic*. God foretold (and threatened) not only what might happen, *potentially*, but, what He knew was positively going to happen, and the results, i.e. judgment.

Notice what God through Moses said at the close of the L-B-C:

"And the LORD said to Moses: "Behold, you will rest with your fathers; and this people will rise and play the harlot with the gods of the foreigners of the land, where they go to be among them, and they will forsake Me and break My covenant which I have made with them. Then My anger shall be aroused against them in that day, and I will forsake them, and I will hide My face from them, and they shall be devoured. And many evils and troubles shall befall them, so that they will say in that day, 'Have not these evils come upon us because our God is not among us?' And I will surely hide My face in that day because of all the evil which they have done, in that they have turned to other gods. "Now therefore, write down this song for yourselves, and teach it to the children of Israel; put it in their mouths, that this song may be a witness for Me against the children of Israel" (Deuteronomy 31:16-19).

So, YHVH delivered the L-B-C and then told Moses that the time was coming when Israel would forsake the covenant and He would have to apply those covenant sanctions. This is *prophecy*. Notice how this played out in Israel's history.

The law of Blessings and Cursings was based squarely on the Sinaitic Covenant. God said that failure to keep the feast days, including Sabbath, the moral mandates, would result in the application of the covenant curses. We see this even in the prophetic books. Notice how the Assyrian invasion and destruction of the ten northern tribes is specifically cast in the framework of their failure to keep Torah. Let me illustrate this with a chart:

Deuteronomy 28-30	Amos 4-5
28:22 Blast with Blight	4:9- Curse of Blight
No Bread 28:37	4:6– Bread Taken Away
Plagues 28:27, 60	4:10 - God would bring the plagues on Israel
Overthrow As Sodom 29:23	4:11 - Israel to be overthrown like Sodom
Captivity 28:64/ 28:25	5:1-5 - They were about to be taken into captivity
No rain, 28:23	4:7 - God would shut up the heavens
Captivity 28:64	5:27 - I will send you into captivity

From these comparisons it is easily seen that the Assyrian invasion and destruction of the ten northern tribes was the application of Mosaic Covenant sanctions– the L-B-C– on Israel.

Furthermore, the invasion is described as the coming of the Lord:

"For behold, the LORD is coming out of His place; He will come down And tread on the high places of the earth. The mountains will melt under Him, And the valleys will split Like wax before the fire, Like waters poured down a steep place. All this is for the transgression of Jacob And for the sins of the house of Israel. What is the transgression of Jacob? Is it not Samaria? And what are the high places of Judah? Are they not Jerusalem? " Therefore I will make Samaria a heap of ruins in the field, Places for planting a vineyard; I will pour down her stones into the valley, And I will uncover her foundations. All her carved images shall be beaten to pieces, And all her pay as a harlot shall be burned with the fire; All her idols I will lay desolate, For she gathered it from the pay of a harlot, And they shall return to the pay of a harlot" (Micah 1:2-7).

So, Israel violated Torah, just as God said she would. As a result of that apostasy, YHVH came out of heaven against Israel, taking her into captivity, in application of the L-B-C.

Just as God punished the ten northern tribes for her violation of Torah, note that in Jeremiah 7 God likewise threatened Judah and Jerusalem with covenant wrath. And what is so interesting about this is that the sins of Jerusalem are the sins delineated in Malachi 3:5:

"Thus says the LORD of hosts, the God of Israel: "Amend your ways and your doings, and I will cause you to dwell in this place. Do not trust in these lying words, saying, 'The temple of the LORD, the temple of the LORD, the temple of the LORD are these.' "For if you thoroughly amend your ways and your doings, if you thoroughly execute judgment between a man and his neighbor, if you do not oppress the stranger, the fatherless, and the widow, and do not shed innocent blood in this place, or walk after other gods to your hurt, then I will cause you to dwell in this place, in the land that I gave to your fathers forever and ever." (Jeremiah 7:1-7).

The problem was that Jerusalem was committing those very sins (v. 8-10)– in violation of Exodus 22:21f, Deuteronomy 27:19f. Therefore, just as God said in Exodus, He would punish them by the edge of the sword. Once again, this is the application of Mosaic Covenant sanctions.

So, both the Assyrian and the Babylonian captivities are specifically posited as a result of covenant violation and the imposition of the L-B-C. Just like the Assyrian invasion was called the Day of the Lord's coming out of heaven to tread on the mountains, the Chaldean invasion was likewise called, "The Great Day of the Lord" (Zephaniah 1-2).

110

Not only were the Mosaic Covenant sanctions applied to Israel in the Assyrian and Babylonian captivities but, God predicted that in Israel's last days, in her latter end, those same sanctions would come to bear on her.

Notice Deuteronomy 31:29:

"For I know that after my death you will become utterly corrupt, and turn aside from the way which I have commanded you. And evil will befall you in the latter days, because you will do evil in the sight of the LORD, to provoke Him to anger through the work of your hands."

So, YHVH gave the L-B-C and then, in direct relationship with that Covenant, He said that in the last days Israel would apostatize and fill the measure of her sin. As a result, "evil will befall you in the latter days."

This terminology of evil coming on Israel as a result of her violation of Torah is taken directly from the L-B-C. Three times (a three fold witness) God said that in the coming generations when Israel would sin that the covenant sanctions would come on them (28:15, 45; 30:1). Enter John the Baptizer, once again.

Remember that in Malachi 3 we see YHVH's declaration that He was going to come in judgment of Israel for committing the identical crimes found in Exodus, Deuteronomy, the sins that led directly to the Assyrian and Babylonian invasions, *there is no way to posit that judgment outside the Mosaic Covenant framework.* This means, unequivocally, that since John was Elijah proclaiming the judgment of Malachi 3, that John was predicting the imminent coming of the Great and Terrible Day of the Lord in the application of Mosaic Covenant Sanctions. And, to once again drive the point home, there was no "Great and Terrible Day of the Lord" between John and the cross, which is where we are told that Torah passed away. This is an insurmountable problem for that view of Torah. Here is prophecy and Torah, here is *Torah and Telos*, linked inseparably.

So, we have indisputable proof that,

A.) The Law of Blessings and Cursings was "the law."

B.) The L-B-C was "the covenant."

C.) It was "the Law of Moses."

D.) It was prophetic.

What this means is that until *God's covenant* with Israel was fully accomplished not one jot or tittle would pass from Torah.

It means that until *"the law of Moses"* was fully accomplished– all of it, not one jot or one tittle would pass away.

It means that until *the Law of Blessings and Cursings*– "the law" was completely fulfilled, not one iota of the Law would become invalid.

It means that until *the prophecy* of (at least) the application of the L-B-C in Israel's last days was completed, when she had filled the measure of her sin, then not on particle, not a single aspect of the minutia of the law, would cease to be binding on Israel.

Now, in regard to the latter point, remember John's role as Elijah, to prepare for and proclaim the coming of the Great and Terrible Day of the Lord, which would be in application of the sanctions of the L-B-C.

Since, as we have seen, The Day of the Lord did not occur between the ministry of John and the cross, then Torah either failed before and without being accomplished– which is precisely what Jesus said could not happen– or, as we have seen, John (Elijah's) prophecy was fulfilled after John and after Pentecost. And this is precisely what we find. I will make this brief, but, this is important.

Elijah and Revelation

Take a look again at Malachi 3:1-3:

"Behold, I send My messenger, And he will prepare the way before Me. And the Lord, whom you seek, Will suddenly come to His temple, Even the Messenger of the covenant, In whom you delight. Behold, He is coming," Says the LORD of hosts. "But who can endure the day of His coming? And who can stand when He appears? For He is like a refiner's fire And like launderers' soap."

Note that Malachi foretold the coming of the Lord and posed the challenging question: "Who can stand when He appears?" The Lord would come like fire, said the prophet. Then, in chapter 4 the prophet continues the discussion of that Day that would burn like fire. He says it would be the Day when the Lord would judge the wicked and burn them like stubble. This is the Day of Judgment.

Notice now Revelation 6:12f which describes the answer to the prayer of the martyrs under the altar, who cried out for vindication and for vengeance on their persecutors:

"I looked when He opened the sixth seal, and behold, there was a great earthquake; and the sun became black as sackcloth of hair, and the moon became like blood. And the stars of heaven fell to the earth, as a fig tree drops its late figs when it is shaken by a mighty wind. Then the sky receded as a scroll when it is rolled up, and every mountain and island was moved out of its place. And the kings of the earth, the great men, the rich men, the commanders, the mighty men, every slave and every free man, hid themselves in the caves and in the rocks of the mountains, and said to the mountains and rocks, 'Fall on us and hide us from the face of Him who sits on the throne and from the wrath of the Lamb! For the great day of His wrath has come, and who is able to stand?"

★ This is the coming of the Great and Terrible Day of the Lord of Malachi 4:5-6– of which John the Baptizer was the herald and sign.

★ We have here the Day of the Lord that would burn like fire– that John the Baptizer spoke of, as Elijah.

★ We have here the citation and promise of the fulfillment also of Isaiah 2-4, a prediction of the last days vindication of the martyrs, at the Day of the Lord (Isaiah 2-4).

★ We have here the prediction of the Great Day of the Lord when no one could stand before Him, which is the Day of the Lord of Malachi 3-4. The Day that John the Baptizer proclaimed.

★ We have (in Revelation) the refining of the remnant of Israel (chapter 7, 14) to be a kingdom of priests (1:5) just as the Day of the Lord of Malachi would purify the new priesthood of "Levi" to offer sacrifices to God.[151]

★ We have here the prediction of the imminent (to John the Baptizer, and even more imminent to John the apostle in Revelation) fulfillment of Malachi.

Watch what this means:

---

[151] Compare the similar motifs in 1 Peter. The apostle speaks of the refining of their faith– he writes to the *diaspora of Israel*– (1:5f) so that they, as a new, spiritual priesthood, in fulfillment of God's OT promises to Israel, might offer up spiritual sacrifices, acceptable to God (1 Peter 2:5f). While other prophecies certainly lie behind these motifs, Malachi is clearly echoed here.

The coming of the Lord in Revelation 6:12-17 is the coming of the Lord foretold in Malachi 3-4.

The coming of the Lord foretold in Malachi 3-4 would be the coming of the Lord in the application of Mosaic Covenant wrath– i.e. the application of the Law of Blessings and Cursings.

Therefore, the coming of the Lord in Revelation 6:12-17 is the coming of the Lord in the application of Mosaic Covenant wrath– i.e. the application of the Law of Blessings and Cursings

Very clearly, the implications of this are profound.

If the Day of the Lord of Revelation 6 is indeed the Day of the Lord of Malachi, then here is what is demanded:

➜ If that Day has not come, *then Torah – all of it – remains valid now*, and will remain valid until that Day arrives. Remember, you cannot apply any of the promises or sanctions of a law / covenant that has been annulled.

➜ If that Day came in AD 70, which conforms to the undeniable focus of Revelation, then the Law of Moses, the L-B-C remained valid until that time.

➜ What is undeniable is that the Day of the Lord foretold by Malachi, and John as Elijah, did not occur after John the Baptizer, but before the cross. So, unless we want to posit the failure of the prediction of Malachi– and John the Baptizer as Elijah– then we must find the most logical explanation for this dilemma. And no other event better conforms to the imminence of the Day of Wrath foretold by John, and the judgment of Jerusalem in AD 70. Of course, as just noted, this is therefore irrefutable proof that Torah and Israel were not left behind at the cross.

The Prophets Were Called The Law

What should be more than apparent from the material above is that the Law of Moses was both "the law" and, just as Jesus' words "the law and the prophets prophesied" indicate, the Law of Moses was also, fundamentally prophetic. Prophecy, i.e. the L-B-C, was "the law." The Law of Moses foretold the events of Israel's last days, thus, "the law" was prophecy.

114

This point, along with the previous one, is critical to the issue before us. Since the OT prophetic corpus was called "the law" then any attempt to say that part of the law could pass while the prophetic element remains valid is falsified.

One thing that is overlooked or ignored by those who claim that part of Torah has passed but that the prophetic element remains is that the very part of the Law of Moses that they insist has passed *was itself intrinsically prophetic*. This is an undeniable fact. Let me drive this home.

No one, and I mean *no one*, denies that the Temple cultus established by JHVH was typological. It foreshadowed, anticipated and foretold (prophesied!) "Better things to come" (Colossians 2:14-16). Now, catch this: Paul says that the New Moons, Feast Days and the Sabbaths (which everyone agrees were "the law) were predictive.

Absolutely no one denies that the New Moons, feast days and Sabbaths were "the law." But, those festal praxis were, *intrinsically prophetic*! Thus, "the law" of the New Moons, feast days and Sabbaths *prophesied*.

Jesus' declaration that not one jot or one tittle would pass from "the law" until it was all fulfilled must of logical necessity therefore include those feast days.

Thus, not one iota of "the law" including the ceremonial and sacrificial typological feast days would pass until all that they foretold was fully accomplished.

Does anyone in evangelical Christianity doubt or deny that the Passover feast and sacrifice pointed to Jesus? No. Does anyone doubt that the Feast of Unleavened Bread, Feast of Weeks and Pentecost pointed to Jesus' resurrection and the establishment of the church in Acts 2? No.

So, here we have a fundamental part of Exodus, Leviticus and Deuteronomy, "the law" given at Sinai / Horeb, and those mandates,

those ceremonial, sacrificial feast days were prophetic to the core.
Thus, just as Jesus said, "all the prophets *and the law* prophesied until
John" (Matthew 11:12, my emphasis).

Let me express my argument succinctly:

**Not one iota of "the law" would pass until it was all fully
accomplished (Matthew 5:18).**

But, the New Moons, Feast Days and Sabbaths were "the law."

**The New Moons Feast Days and Sabbaths, i.e. "the law" were
likewise prophetic.**

**Thus, until every jot and tittle of the New Moons Feast Days and
Sabbaths was fully accomplished, not one iota of "the law"
would pass.**

Without any doubt whatsoever, the law prophesied, and prophecy
was "the law."

Not only were those ceremonial, sacrificial mandates undeniably "the
law," it should likewise be noted that those cultic sacrifices were
inextricably part of "the covenant." I know of no one that would even
attempt to deny this. It is axiomatic. The Mosaic Law was the Mosaic
Covenant. The cultic, festal calendar was the Mosaic Law. Therefore,
the cultic, festal calendar was the covenant.

Since the Mosaic Law was the Mosaic Covenant, and since the
ceremonial, sacrificial cultus was the Mosaic Law, it therefore follows
that the ceremonial, sacrificial cultus was part and parcel, part of the
warp and woof, of the Mosaic Covenant.

What this means, to express things in a slightly different manner, is
that until the ceremonial, sacrificial cultus was fully accomplished,
bringing to full realization that which was foreshadowed and promised
in those New Moons, feast days and Sabbaths, then *God's covenant
with Israel would remain intact.*[152] You cannot claim that God left

---

[152] This point is driven home even more with
consideration of *the Sabbath as God's covenant with Israel.*
To express it in simple form: The Sabbath was a covenant sign
between YHVH and Israel. Sabbath was "the law." Sabbath

116

Israel and Torah behind at the cross, therefore, and yet affirm the post cross fulfillment of Israel's covenantal festal calendar– which included the eschatological final three feasts. If that which the ceremonial feast days foretold is still unfulfilled, then Torah, God's covenant with Israel, remains valid. This is inescapable.

You cannot– logically- affirm that "the law" i.e the sacrificial and ceremonial New Moons, feast days and Sabbaths, have been annulled, and then affirm the yet future fulfillment of what those cultic praxis foreshadowed and foretold. If those cultic feast days are annulled, then either what they foretold has been accomplished– The Judgment, Atonement, Resurrection– or, what they foreshadowed has been nullified. If the promises are valid, then Torah is valid.

Yet, all three futurist paradigms tell us that the Mosaic Law was removed at the cross.[153] They affirm that the sacrifices and the feast days have been abrogated, but, that the very thing that those final feast days foreshadowed and promised, i.e. judgment, salvation and resurrection, have not yet been fully accomplished. Do you see the problem? This is a massive issue. It is the elephant in the room that no one is even discussing.

---

foreshadowed the eschatological resurrection. Therefore, until the Sabbath was fully realized at the eschatological resurrection, God's covenant with Israel would remain intact. Non-Sabbatarians are not dealing with this thorny issue in any substantive manner. I will be discussing this entire issue of the Sabbath in another volume in this series.

[153] As noted, this is the argument of (preterist) Kurt Simmons in our written debate. He claimed that the law, the ceremonial, sacrificial element of Torah, was removed at the cross, but that the resurrection– foreshadowed and promised in that law– did not occur until AD 70. This is patently a violation of Jesus' words.

So, to reiterate and summarize, Jesus said that the law and the prophets prophesied. We have demonstrated beyond any doubt that in the Jewish vernacular and in the Biblical usage, the term "the law" was referent to the entirety of what is commonly called the Old Testament. From Genesis to Malachi, it was all considered and called "the law."

We have also demonstrated that the Mosaic Covenant was "the law." We have seen that "the law" was "the covenant." We have likewise seen that the Law of Blessings and Cursings was called "the law of Moses" and was intrinsically prophetic. Thus, "the law" prophesied, just as Jesus said.

So, "the law" was "the covenant" which prophesied. Clearly therefore, any attempt to sharply dichotomize between the different genres of literature found in Torah, and say that, for instance, the Psalms were not "the law" or that the prophetic books were not called "the law"[154] is simply false.

Finally, we have shown that while all three futurist eschatologies say that the ceremonial and sacrificial aspect of Torah has passed, they then cite the OT for their futurist eschatologies, all the while overlooking the undeniable fact that the OT prophecies of the eschaton were based directly upon, and foreshadowed in, the ceremonial, sacrificial New Moons, Feast Days and Sabbaths.

It is a blatant self contradiction to say on the one hand that those feast days have been annulled and then to anticipate that which those feast days pointed to. If that to which they pointed has not been realized, then the shadows (and cultus) are still binding. You can't affirm the futuricity of what those feast days foretold, without at the same time affirming the abiding validity of the prophetic, ceremonial

---

[154] Remember that we proved earlier in this work where Paul quoted from the Psalms, Jeremiah and Isaiah, and specifically called these books "the law." Those who seek therefore to say that Jesus did not have the prophetic books in mind in Matthew 5 are violating the scriptural use of the term "the law."

and sacrificial feast days.[155] This is unavoidable– and fatal to the futurist views of both Torah and Telos.

It is simply wrong to deny that the term "the law" was referent to the Psalms, the prophets, the Law of Blessings and Cursings– All of what we call the Old Testament.

Thus, the prophetic books were "the law" and Jesus said that not the smallest element of "the law" would pass until it was "ALL" fulfilled.

This demands that until all of what the prophets foretold was fully accomplished that not one iota of Torah would pass.

---

[155] Kurt Simmons, astoundingly, after our debate in which he offered not a word in response to the significance of the feast days, then claimed that all of the feast days– including the Feast of Tabernacles (i.e the resurrection) was fulfilled in Jesus' ministry, because after all, John said "the Word tabernacled with us." Thus, for Simmons, the Feast of Tabernacles did not, after all, foreshadow the eschatological harvest, but, *the Incarnation of Jesus*. This historically unprecedented "argument" simply illustrates the desperation and lengths to which men will go to uphold their preconceived ideas.

WHAT DOES *ALL* MEAN

Jesus' words "not one jot or one tittle shall pass from the law until it is all fulfilled" surely seem, by any natural reading, to demand the fulfillment of all of Torah. After all, does not the very term "jot and tittle" include everything in Torah? If the "jots and tittles" refer to the entirety of the Law of Moses, then how can we, logically, deny that "the Law" which was comprised of all those "jots and tittles" not be a comprehensive term? And when Jesus said "all" had to be fully accomplished, does not the comprehensive term "all" not demand total fulfillment of the entire Old Covenant?

In spite of the seeming clarity of Jesus' words, it is abundantly clear from what we have seen above that there are those who claim that the words do not demand a total fulfillment of Torah. Rather, it is claimed *all* that Jesus meant was that his passion was *all* that was required for Torah to pass. (Excuse the puns with the use of "all"!)[156]

We would quickly note that the word "all" can be used in a limited sense. No one denies this. However, if "all" is to be understood in a limited sense, the context must *demand* and *define* the limited definition of all. We are not free to limit the definition of "all" based on our presuppositional theology. More on this momentarily.

As we noted above, there are several "explanations" offered to counter or redefine the word "all" in Matthew 5:17-18. Let me reiterate and address those objections here.

---

[156] It is interesting to say the least that in some circles it is being affirmed that the "some" in Daniel 12:2 excludes the text from being predictive of the eschatological resurrection. After all, we are told, "some" cannot mean "all." Of course this overlooks the possibility that "some" is being used as a Hebraism. Nonetheless, those who make the claim then turn around and say that the "all" in Matthew 5:17-18 cannot mean "all" even though there is absolutely no contextual qualifier present.

#1 All Does Not Mean All Because...

"Jesus only meant to say that *when the Law had fulfilled its purpose* it would pass. He was not saying that all of Torah had to be fulfilled."

Response: I suppose the simplest response to this objection would be, if this is what Jesus meant, why did he not say it that way? In essence, this explanation says that when Jesus had fulfilled the purpose of the law, then the law would pass. This is, for all practical purposes sake a self defeating argument. This argument says that the parts that were unfulfilled, *did not have Christ as their purpose*. Yet, Christ was the goal (*telos*) of "the law" (Romans 10:4). He was the goal of *the entire law*, not just part of it.

Paul said that the Law was given to "bring us to Christ" (Galatians 3:23-24). Did he mean that the Law only lasted until the birth of Jesus? After all, one might argue that this is when Christ came. Yet, no one takes that position. So, the coming of Christ in view in Galatians, in regard to the Law fulfilling its purpose, cannot be taken in an atomistic, simplistic view. There is something deeper indicated in Paul's terminology of the coming of Christ. Notice a few things.

Paul said, "before (the) faith came, we were kept under guard by the law, kept for the faith which should afterward be revealed" (Galatians 3:23). It is important to honor the use of the definite articles in the verse. Paul says they were under the law, in anticipation of the coming of "the faith." This means that the purpose of the law was to bring Israel to "the faith"- the New Covenant "system."

Did "the faith" i.e. the objective system of the gospel, fully arrive at the cross? Patently not. Nor was it fully arrived at Pentecost. Paul's distinctive role as an apostle was the transformation from the Old Covenant to the New (2 Corinthians 3:16- 4:1-3). That is, Paul's role was to bring in the fulfillment of the purpose of the law– the full arrival of "the faith." That system was in the process of being revealed at the very time that Paul wrote Galatians.

So, since the purpose of the law was to bring in the completed New Covenant system of "the faith," then since the New Covenant was not completed at the cross / Pentecost, then the argument that all Jesus had to do was to fulfill the purpose of the law for Torah to pass is self defeating. It actually affirms the idea that Torah could not pass until all

of its prophecies– inclusive of the revelation of the New Covenant–
was fulfilled.

2 All Does Not Mean All Because...
Jesus was referring to the cultic practices passing away, when he would fulfill the typology of the sacrificial system in his death.

Response: Is it not strange that the cultic observances of Torah are not even mentioned in Matthew 5, and yet, we are supposed to believe that Jesus was saying none of Torah would pass until the Temple cultus was abrogated? Should Jesus not have at least mentioned, *in some way*, which aspect, which jots and tittles, would pass when they were fulfilled?

DeMar, writing against the dispensational emphasis on a future restoration of the Temple, insists that the festal calendar of Israel stands fulfilled. He notes that the New Testament describes Jesus as the fulfillment of every element of the Old Covenant shadows, feasts included (Passover, Unleavened Bread, First fruits, Pentecost): "And beginning with Moses and with all the prophets, (Jesus) explained to (His disciples) the things concerning Himself in all the Scriptures. . .. That all the things which are written about (Jesus) in the Law of Moses and the Prophets and the Psalms must be fulfilled" (24:27, 44). Earlier in Luke's Gospel we read "that all things which are written" about the end of the Old Covenant were "fulfilled" (21:22).[157] Jesus is the "lamb of God" (John 1:29, 36), the temple (2:29), the bread from heaven (6:48), the high priest (Heb. 5:10), and the Rock (1 Cor. 10:4)."[158]

---

[157] It is more than a little interesting that DeMar cites Luke 21:22 as the terminus for the fulfillment of all things, and yet, likewise seeks to point to the cross as that point of fulfillment. Luke 21:22 refers not to the cross, but to the events of the Jewish War of AD 66-70, as DeMar himself believes. So, DeMar is rather subtly indicating AD 70 as the point of the actual fulfillment of Torah– which he does in fact seem to believe, or, he is being self contradictory.

[158] http://americanvision.org/5146/defending-dispensationalism-at-all-costs/

As we have seen above, DeMar is emphatic in declaring: "One of the first things a Christian must learn in interpreting the Bible is to pay attention to the time texts. Failing to recognize the proximity of a prophetic event will distort its intended meaning. The New Testament clearly states that the 'end of all things' was at hand for those who first read 1 Peter 4:7; that is, the Old Covenant with its types and shadows was about to pass away." (*Madness*, 1994, 27).

As we have seen earlier, Gentry says, "Christ has surpassed the legal foreshadows and rituals of the Old Testament."[159]

The problem with this objection is that those who affirm that the cultic, sacrificial aspect of Torah passed at the cross are completely overlooking the fact that the cultic, festal, sacrificial aspect of Torah was intrinsically prophetic. And not only were those elements of Torah prophetic, *they foreshadowed the eschatological consummation*.

But, here is what happens in the non-dispensational world.

☞ We are told that the sacrificial cultus was annulled.

☞ *However*, the "moral code" remains valid. Well, that is, except the seventh day cultic, ceremonial Sabbath that lies embedded within the "moral code."

☞ *Then* we are told that the eschatological prophecies found in Torah– and specifically the eschatological feast days, which includes *all of the Sabbaths* -- likewise remain unrealized, unfulfilled.

---

[159] Kenneth Gentry in *House Divided the Breakup of Dispensational Theology*, by Greg Bahnsen and Kenneth Gentry, (Tyler, Tx., Institute for Christian Economics, 1989)40. Gentry thus ignores Jesus' emphatic words that "not one jot or tittle shall pass from the law until it is all fulfilled." He wants to abrogate the ceremonial part of Torah, and keep the Decalogue, while ignoring the fact that the Sabbath is firmly embedded in the Decalogue! Thus, part of Torah could pass when part of it was fulfilled! As David Chilton pointed out in 1997, at a prophecy conference in Oklahoma City that I helped organize, the very verses that postmillennialists appeal to for support are actually their downfall! (Chilton's speech, along with the other presentations at that conference is available from me).

123

Do you see the problem? If ever there was a, "some will pass when some is fulfilled" view of Matthew 5 this is it. This position therefore affirms that what Jesus was saying was that a portion of the law would pass away, while the majority of the law will remain.

Bahnsen affirmed, "So long as the world lasted it (the law's) authority was to be permanent. Every single stroke of the law must be seen by the Christian as applicable to this very age between the advents of Christ." (See just below for more on Bahnsen).

Do you see what this statement and theology does? It breaks Torah up into ceremonial, prophetic and moral, claiming that the ceremonial was not prophetic. This is of course, patently false, as we have seen. And this brings us back to Jesus' words.

Notice carefully that Jesus said, "not one jot or one tittle will pass from the law until it is all fulfilled. Focus on the "jot and tittle."

As Bahnsen correctly notes: "The exhaustive particulars of God's law have 'an imperishable validity for all time.' The double negative associated with the minutia of the law in regard to their invalidation is (with the aorist subjunctive) the most definite form of negation concerning the future: it is also the classical way of strengthening the negative. The details of the law will by no means become invalid until heaven and earth pass away." (*Theonomy*, 2002, 80).

When Jesus said "not one jot or one tittle shall pass" and then said "until it is all fulfilled" then grammatically, the "all is fulfilled" refers directly back to the "jots and tittles." Thus, Jesus asservation that not one jot or one tittle shall pass until it is all fulfilled, logically means that he was saying "not one jot or one tittle shall pass from the law until every jot and every tittle is fulfilled." Honoring the language of the text therefore, precludes any idea that Jesus was saying, "when some of the sacrificial elements of Torah have been fulfilled, then some of the law will pass, but some will remain valid. You cannot have "all" refer to anything other than the "not one jot or one tittle."

One cannot help but be struck with the inconsistency of the Theonomic view of Torah. In his quote, Bahnsen correctly notes that Jesus was speaking comprehensively of the, "exhaustive particulars of the minutia" of Torah. Thus, *nothing*, not one single iota, not one single particular, not one single command, or, therefore, *not one single cultic, sacrificial, ceremony* (read that "prophetic) jot or tittle of the law would pass until "the details of the law" are fully realized.

In spite of Bahnsen and the Theonomic verbiage about the absolute necessity for the abiding validity of the minutia of Torah "until (literal, DKP) heaven and earth pass away", the Theonomists then turn around and, as noted, tell us that the cultic aspects of the Sabbath (and the Sabbaths), has passed.

They tell us that the ceremonial aspects of the Sabbath have been annulled– replaced by the typological "Christian Sabbath."[160]

They tell us that physical circumcision– a foundational "jot and tittle" of Torah, has been annulled.

They tell us we no longer have to offer the bloody sacrifices and make the annual trip to Jerusalem, as demanded by Torah, because those sacrifices have been fulfilled– that part of the law removed.

They tell us that the land of Israel and Jerusalem have lost their theological and covenantal significance.

They tell us that the Temple in Jerusalem was left desolate and superceded because God Himself fulfilled its typological significance in Christ.

They tell us that the Aaronic priesthood, so foundationally important to the entire world of Israel, has been abrogated. They tell us.... well, you get the picture, don't you?

Isn't that an awful lot of "jots and tittles" that have passed, in spite of the Theonomic insistence that not the slightest minutia, not a single one of the "exhaustive particulars" will pass until the end of human history? To say the least, this is theological double-speak.

---

[160] Here is a strange thing indeed. Per the Theonomists, the typological Sabbath has been replaced by *another typological Sabbath.* Yet, Paul said Christ is the body– the reality– not another shadow, not another type. What is the justification for claiming, as the Dominionist view demands, that the typological OT Sabbath was replaced by the anti-typical "Christian" Sabbath, *which then turns into the typological Sabbath?*

On the one hand, Theonomists insist that every jot and every tittle of Torah had to be fulfilled for Torah to pass. Then they tell us that the Law– every stroke-- will remain valid until the end of time. Then they turn around and say that a *plethora* of the jots and tittles of the Law– the entire Temple cultus--has indeed passed. To call this logically inconsistent is to understate the case.

The bottom line is that one cannot decree that some of the cultic, sacrificial elements of Torah have passed, and then claim that some of them, the eschatological feast days, remain unfulfilled. If any of the ceremonial feast days were or are not fulfilled, then every single "exhaustive particular" of the Law remains in force.

As should be evident, all three futurist eschatologies have a massive problem here, for all three futurist paradigms affirm the cessation of the ceremonial cultus of Torah, and then they appeal to the OT for support for their eschatology. They thus affirm the passing of some of Torah, and the abiding validity of some of the jots and tittles. This is an undeniable violation of Jesus' words.

3 All Does Not Mean All Because...
The Bible affirms that Jesus did fulfill all things when he died on the cross.

"After this, Jesus, knowing that all things were now accomplished, that the Scripture might be fulfilled, said, "I thirst!" Now a vessel full of sour wine was sitting there; and they filled a sponge with sour wine, put it on hyssop, and put it to His mouth. So when Jesus had received the sour wine, He said, "It is finished!" And bowing His head, He gave up His spirit" (John 19:28-31).

126

Response:

This objection is a classic example of reading too much into a text. Because it says that Jesus knew that "all things were now accomplished", it is assumed that it refers to all of Torah. That is, it is assumed that all of the law that had to be fulfilled for the law to pass was now accomplished. There are numerous problems with this assumption.

First, it projects a limited "all" onto a text where there is no limitation. This is an illegitimate transfer of context. When one context defines the "all" in view, that does not mean that a limited definition can therefore be imposed on another text, where no limitation is given. As Bahnsen noted, there is no definite article in the text of Matthew 5 to specify which jots and tittles would pass. There is no contextual limitation of the "all" as is found in John 19 (or Luke 18:30f).

Second, the "all" of John 19 is patently all that was foretold concerning Jesus' sacrificial *death*. Would anyone claim that all prophecies of Jesus' *resurrection* were not essential for the fulfilling of all things?

Third, on this note, observe also that Jesus' death was to make the atonement. Yet, the atonement was basically a three-step *process*. It was not a stand alone, singular act of killing the sacrificial animal. To suggest otherwise is clearly a violation of history and Torah.

The second step in the atonement process was entry into the Most Holy Place by the High Priest, as he took the blood of the sacrifice before the divine Ark of the Covenant, and the Mercy Seat, there to offer it to YHVH. Technically speaking, the sacrifice was not even "made" until it was offered there, in the Most Holy Place.

The third and final act of the atonement process was when the High Priest returned from that Most Holy Place. His appearance from that sacred realm signaled that YHVH accepted the sacrifice and that Israel was accepted in Covenant fellowship for another year.

The writer of Hebrews makes a point of following this pattern in the work of Jesus. Christ had appeared to put away sin by the sacrifice of himself (Hebrews 9.26). He had entered the MHP there to offer that sacrifice and "prepare a place" for the congregation (cf. Hebrews 9:24). And, in fulfillment of the types and shadows of Torah, he would appear again the second time, apart from sin, to those who were eagerly looking for him (Hebrews 9.28).

Notice that in Hebrews 10:1f, after speaking of Christ appearing at the climax of the atonement process, the author of Hebrews says, "for, the law, having a shadow of good things (about) to come..." The word "for" in 10.1 links it inseparably with 9.28 and gives the reason why Christ had to come again. Christ had to come again because the Day of Atonement found in the law was a type and shadow of his coming.

So, *Christ had to return from the MHP to fulfill Torah.* Now, if it was necessary for Christ to appear again to fulfill the law, then it is impossible to say that Torah had passed away at the cross. I think Holwerda expresses it well in regard to the fulfillment of types: "When fulfillment happens, the institutions that were types or symbols of that reality are no longer necessary. They are displaced by the reality they symbolize."[161]

If types are no longer necessary when they were fulfilled, and if Christ's high priestly actions were typological– which is irrefutably true– then until Christ's appearing "the second time" at the climax of the Atonement praxis was absolutely essential for the fulfillment– and the passing– of Torah.

If Christ had to "appear again a second time" in order to fulfill the types and shadows of Torah, as Hebrews 9:28-10:1 undeniably says, then it is patently false to say that the law passed away at the cross. Christ could not "fulfill" dead, irrelevant, annulled types and shadows.

Those who insist that Torah passed at the cross not only appeal to John 19.28 but, they then appeal to Jesus' words, "It is finished" in verse 31 to suggest that Jesus was saying that Torah was ended. This suggestion completely overlooks the Passover sacrifice and what was taking place in Jesus' death.

It is un-necessary to document here that Jesus' passion occurred at the time of the Passover. What I want to note here is that when we take

---

[161] David Holwerda, *Jesus and Israel: One Covenant or Two?*, (Grand Rapids, Eerdmans, 1995) 75.

the Passover typology into consideration, Jesus' words, "It is finished" were not intended to speak of the end of the law. Rather, he was declaring that the Passover sacrifice itself was finished.

The parallels between Jesus' passion and the Passover are incredible. Numerous authors have outlined those parallels, and those can be found on Internet with a Google search.

As only one example, notice the following from Ted Montgomery: "According to Bible historian Joseph Good, the Passover lamb in the temple was bound to the altar at about 9:00 a.m. (3) Similarly, "It was the third hour when they crucified [Jesus]" (Mark 15:25); that is, it was the third hour of daylight, or about 9:00 a.m. Darkness came over the land (not explainable by a solar eclipse, because there was a full moon rather than a new moon) from about the sixth to the ninth hour (noon to 3:00 p.m.); and it was about 3:00 p.m. that Jesus died (Luke 23:44,45a,46)—the same time that the sacrificial Passover lamb in the temple was slaughtered. As the high priest killed the lamb, he would have announced, "It is finished." It is no accident that, on the cross a few miles away, Jesus' last words also were, "It is finished" (John 19:30a)."[162]

Now, if Montgomery is correct in his parallels, and one can easily see how agreeable they are, then Jesus' "It is finished" cannot be construed as a comment on the end of Torah. He was in fact acting as the High Priest, *declaring the fulfillment of the typological Passover sacrifice.*

The implications of that declaration are significant. The Passover was the first of the first four of Israel's feast days. It was followed by the Unleavened Bread, Feast of Weeks and then Pentecost, fifty days later.

4 All Does Not Mean All Because...
"The Law" refers to the cultic, sacrificial element of Torah, but has nothing to do with the Decalogue, i.e. the moral law.

Response:

162

http://www.tedmontgomery.com/bblovrvw/c_4a.html

We have already falsified and negated this argument above, in our demonstration that all elements of the Tanakh, the Old Testament, are referred to as "the law." There is simply no justification for divorcing the cultic, ceremonial elements of "the law" from the moral elements of "the law." This is a specious and un-Biblical position.

The language of Matthew 5:17f will not allow the objection under consideration. Where is there any reference to the cultic aspect of Torah in Matthew 5? Where does Jesus indicate he is speaking of the sacrificial system that will pass, but exclude other tenets and elements from abrogation? Should we not have some kind of actual textual evidence to support this claim?

Jesus' words are comprehensive: "not one jot or one tittle of the law" cannot be limited to the Temple cultus.

But, let's consider this objection from another angle, shall we? Those who offer this objection are not thinking of the implications of their own claim. Notice the implications of what they are saying:

Not one jot or one tittle of the (sacrificial and ceremonial) law would pass until it was all fulfilled.

But, the ceremonial and sacrificial law foretold the eschatological day of judgment, final salvation and the resurrection.

Therefore, until the eschatological day of judgment, final salvation and the resurrection were– or are– fulfilled, not one jot or one tittle of the (sacrificial and ceremonial) law would (or will) pass. until it was all fulfilled.

Do you see what has happened? By seeking to limit the definition of "the law" to the sacrificial, ceremonial part of Torah, those who make the objection actually wind up affirming the abiding validity of the Old Testament, for those very students tell is that the final judgment, salvation and the resurrection have not yet been fulfilled. But, if those eschatological elements of Torah have not been fulfilled, then the ceremonial and sacrificial, cultic feast days remain valid.

Of course, we are told that the cultic feast days were abolished, but, the eschaton has not yet come. This is, to understate the case, clearly a violation of Jesus' words. To say that the ceremonial feast days could be annulled without the realization of what they foreshadowed is a direct perversion of Jesus' words.

Futurists who define "the law" in Matthew 5:17-18 as the sacrificial and ceremonial elements of Torah, and affirm that is what was to pass away when fulfilled, *are tacitly affirming the abiding validity of the Temple system.*
Jesus said none of the law– the sacrificial cultus per the objection– would pass until it was all fulfilled.
But, "the law" typified and foretold the Day of Judgment, final salvation and the resurrection.
Therefore, until the final realization of the Day of Judgment, final salvation and the resurrection, i.e. the fulfillment of "the law" not one single iota of the cultus of Israel will pass away!
The futurists have thus nullified their own argument!

In my formal written debate with (preterist) Kurt Simmons he argued that the ceremonial aspect of Torah was removed at the cross. However, he then claimed, and agreed, that the resurrection did not occur until AD 70.[163] This is total failure to consider Israel's cultic world as eschatological foreshadowing, and the necessity that those feast days be fulfilled at the parousia and resurrection, before they could pass away.

Likewise, in numerous formal written and public debates[164] my amillennial opponents have made this same argument, without realizing the implications of what they are saying.

---

[163] Preston - Simmons Debate: *The End of Torah, At The Cross or AD 70?* Available from my websites.

[164] See for instance the McDonald - V - Preston written debate, archived on both my websites.

I think Bahnsen correctly apprised the power of Jesus' words, and the folly of commentators who seek to limit the scope of Jesus' "all." He takes note of commentators who seek to limit the "all things" to "Jesus' death on the cross"; "the great facts of Jesus' messianic work"; "until its (Torah) purposes are fulfilled"; "the passing of the Mosaic economy", etc. He calls all of these suggestions *eisegesis.*

He then says,

"A verse like Matthew 5:18, with its unparticularized *panta* (translated as "all" DKP) is prey for such treatment. Now such views might be appropriate pertaining to a verse like Matthew 24:34 from the Olivet Discourse (which reads *panta tauta*), but they are unjustified in Matthew 5:18; the former has a definite referent and antecedent, while the latter does not (it does not even qualify a noun adjacent to it as does Matthew 24:34). Nothing in the context or vocabulary of Matthew 5:18 warrants the induction of speculative meaning; a phrase as colorless and abstract as *panta* should not be particularized, personalized, and steered into this theological preconception. (p. 83)... "In Matthew 5:18 the commencement of the law's passing away is made dependent upon *panta genetai. Panta,* when used without an article or preposition indicates "all things, everything" (as in Matthew 11:27; John 1:3; 3:35; 21:17; 1 Corinthians 2:10; 15:27, 28; Ephesians 1:22a; Revelation 21:5); it is to be taken in this absolutely general sense unless the context dictates some antecedent whole of which panta constitutes the complete parts. It has already been observed that panta does not agree in gender with 'law' nor does it with 'prophets,' 'heaven,' 'earth,' 'jot or tittle" (Bahnsen, *Theonomy*, 2002, 81).

Bahnsen continued: (p. 84) – "Allen's summary of Christ's teaching on the law is to the point: "So long as the world lasted it (the law's) authority was to be permanent.' Every single stroke of the law must be seen by the Christian as applicable to this very age between the advents of Christ."

Hagner concurs with Bahnsen's definition of "all": "The reference to 'the prophets' suggests that the significance of Jesus for the Mosaic Law can only be understood as part of a larger picture, namely the fulfillment of the entire Torah, understood in its broad sense, including the prophets. The entire OT can be referred to as 'the law and the prophets.'"[165]

Bahnsen clearly did not see the implications of his own claims. If every stroke of the law must be seen by the Christian as applicable to this very age between the advents, then one simply cannot argue that many strokes of the law- i.e. the ceremonial, sacrificial cultic praxis of the law, have in fact been nullified.

5 All Does Not Mean All Because...
Jesus said, "I did not come to destroy, but to fulfill." This is taken to mean that Jesus' personal ministry was all that was necessary to fulfill "every jot and every tittle."

Response:
This objection fails to consider the united aspect of the last days. It is so atomistic in its approach that it basically cannot see beyond Jesus' incarnation, while scripture affirms that from Incarnation to Parousia is one organic unity.

Were there differences in the purpose and approach between Jesus' Incarnation and his parousia? Certainly.

Isaiah 42 describes his Incarnation as the time when "a bruised reed shall he not break, and a smoking flax shall he not quench." This is Jesus in his humility "in the body of flesh." But notice that in that same identical context it says "he shall not fail or be discouraged until he has established justice and judgment in the earth." This is clearly a reference to his parousia in judgment.

So, in one text, we find referent to Jesus Incarnation in humility and in the same context a prediction of his coming in judgment. To the mind of Isaiah, guided by the Spirit, there was no disparate dichotomy between the work of Jesus in his Incarnation and his parousia. The one prepared the way for the other. One was the initiation of his work, the other was to be the consummation of his work..

Note something that is really quite simple, yet it answers the objection effective. That is, Jesus did not say he came to fulfill all of

---

[165] Donald Hagner, *Word Biblical Commentary, Matthew*, (Dallas, Word Books 1993)104.

the law and the prophets. Did he say he came to fulfill? Clearly so. That is not in dispute.

However, since the objection claims that Jesus came (the Incarnation) to "fulfill all things," then surely we might expect him to say that he came to fulfill all things. Of course, the language does not support this claim. While Jesus said that he came to fulfill the law and the prophets, he then announced that not one iota of the law (and thus the prophets, as we have seen is demanded by the actual text), would pass until it was all fulfilled. So, again, we are speaking of initiation anticipating consummation.

#6 All Does Not Mean All Because...
Since Jesus said that Torah would not pass away until the heaven and earth passes, this means that the Law remains valid– particularly the Decalogue and Sabbath– until the "end of time." (Sabbatarianism).

Response:
This objection, offered mostly by the Sabbatarians, but note, by Dominion Theonomists as well, winds up being self-defeating.

Note again Bahnsen's claim: "Allen's summary of Christ's teaching on the law is to the point: "So long as the world lasted it (the law's) authority was to be permanent.' Every single stroke of the law must be seen by the Christian as applicable to this very age between the advents of Christ" (*Theonomy*, 2002, 84).

Yet, while maintaining that "every stroke of the law" must be seen by the Christian as applicable until the end of time, Bahnsen nonetheless says: "At the coming of Christ the Sabbath was *purged* of the legalistic accretions brought by the scribes and Pharisees (Luke 13:10-17; 14:1-6; Mark 3:1-6); the Sabbath had suffered corruption at the hands of the autonomous Pharisees just as numerous other moral precepts had (cf. Matthew 5:21-48). Moreover, the *ceremonial and sacrificial aspects* of the Older Testamental cycle of feast days ('new moon, Sabbath year, Jubilee, etc.) along with those cyclic observances of feast days, were 'put out of gear' by Christ's work of redemption. Hence, Colossians 2:16f loosens us from the ceremonial elements of the Sabbath system (the passage seems to be referring specifically to feast *offerings*), and passages such as Romans 15:5f and Galatians 4:10

teach that we need not distinguish these ceremonial days any longer (as the Judaizers were apt to require)" (*Theonomy*, 2002, 226-227– all emphasis his).

Note, Bahnsen says the Sabbath was purged of the legalistic accretions." In words, some of the jots and tittles, some of the strokes of the law, were purged. He says "the ceremonial and sacrificial aspects of the feast days were "put out of gear." That is an awful lot of strokes of the law that were put out of gear! And, he claims that "we need not distinguish ceremonial days any longer." Let's take a quick look at this.

The observance of those ceremonial days was the heart and soul of Israel's Torah. Those ceremonial days included the following:
The weekly Sabbath.
The monthly Sabbaths, i.e. the New Moons.
The seven year Sabbaths.
The 50th year Sabbath (Jubilee).

Then, you had the following ceremonial days, interconnected to all of the above:
The Feast of Passover
The Feast of Unleavened Bread
The Feast of Weeks
The Feast of Pentecost
The Feast of Trumpets
The Day of Atonement
The Feast of Succot- Harvest.

Of course, tied directly to those feast day were the laws of animal sacrifice. Also included were the laws that mandated the annual pilgrimages.

Furthermore, inextricably bound up with Torah was the law of circumcision. Do Dominionists, or Sabbatarians for that matter, say that physical circumcision remains valid? Of course not! Thus, that is more jots and tittles of Torah, some more of the smallest strokes, that have been removed, in spite of the insistence that not the slightest of the minutia of Torah will pass until the end of time.

These things constituted an awful lot of *ceremonial feast jots and tittles*. They were all sacrificial, cultic, and remember, *prophetic*. That

135

is a lot of minutia that have been "put out of gear" per the Dominionists!

So, on the one hand, Bahnsen– and Dominionists[166]– tell us that not a single stroke of the law will pass until the end of time. Then, however, they turn around and tell us that *all the strokes of the law* listed above[167] have been "put out of gear,"; they have been nullified! They no longer apply; yet, we are told, the Law remains forever!![168]

Any way you want to look at it, the ceremonial, festal laws were Torah, they were "the law." It is therefore, the height of inconsistency and self-contradiction to say that all of those jots and tittles have

---

[166] Like Bahnsen, Gentry holds that heaven and earth in Matthew 5:17-18 refers to the literal creation. Thus, Torah remains valid until the end of time. Kenneth Gentry, in *House Divided, the Break-up of Dispensational Theology,* (Tyler, Tx., Institute for Christian Economics, 1989)41. Then, however, like Bahnsen Gentry says parts of Torah have been annulled, "Christ has surpassed the legal foreshadows and rituals of the Old Testament" while at the same time affirming that the Torah remains valid today.

[167] Of course, when it comes down to it, there are a *lot more of the jots and tittles of Torah* that Dominionists say have passed. They agree that the dietary laws of Torah are annulled. They tell us the laws concerning mixing different types of cloth have been removed. One has but to read Leviticus especially, and compare with what Dominionists do not think is still binding, to get the idea that a lot of careful dissection of Torah is going on.

[168] This inconsistency is one of the things that turned David Chilton away from Dominion Theology, to full preterism. Chilton spoke at the 1997 Prophecy Conference in Oklahoma City, which I helped organize. He began his presentation by giving his reasons for becoming a full preterist, and among his reasons was the Theonomist inconsistency in regard to Matthew 5:17-18. Chilton noted that the very passage that Dominionists appeal to for their doctrine actually destroys their doctrine! Copies of that presentation are available from my websites

indeed passed away, and at the same time say that not one stroke of the law will pass until the end of time.

It is complete inconsistency to affirm - as Bahnsen and the Dominionists do– that not one stroke of the law will pass until the end of time, and then turn around and say that the entire sacrificial cultus– with its plethora of laws– has indeed passed away. That is an awful lot of strokes of the law that they say have passed!

Of course, the Sabbatarians seek to avoid this issue by dividing Torah up into "moral commands" i.e the Decalogue, versus the "ceremonial laws" of cultus and sacrifice. However, as we have seen above, scripture simply does not support such a dichotomy. The prophetic books were called the law. The Decalogue was called "the law." The entire Old Testament was called "the law." There is simply no way to justify saying that God removed part of the law but kept part of the law. Let me illustrate the Sabbatarian problem on this.

Remember that the Adventists (I use that term comprehensively) affirm that "the law" was the Decalogue. They tell us that "the law" is eternal, but that the cultic, ceremonial and sacrificial "law of Moses" was done away. This is actually destructive of the Sabbatarian futurist eschatology. Here, in short form, is why.

The last three of Israel's festivals were *all Sabbaths*, as virtually all Adventists agree. This is affirmed by Paul in Colossians 2:14-16. Jesus fulfilled and removed that cultic, festal system, we are told, but, the seventh day Sabbath remains valid and binding. This will not work.

The seventh day Sabbath foreshadowed the final salvation and resurrection, just like the last three feast days– *all Sabbaths*– typified that same eschatological consummation.

In other words, *the seventh day Sabbath and the last three festal Sabbaths pointed to the same thing– resurrection.* How then can it be argued that some of the Sabbaths have been annulled– or even fulfilled– without annulling what they foreshadowed, thereby annulling the seventh day Sabbath and what it foreshadowed as well? All of the Sabbaths were inextricably bound to each other in what they foretold.

It cannot be affirmed, logically, therefore, that some of the Sabbaths were removed, without demanding the removal of all of the Sabbaths. Furthermore, if one argues, as virtually all futurists, including the Sabbatarians do, that the feast days were fulfilled, then this demands that the resurrection, foreshadowed in those festivals, has been *fulfilled*. Remember, none would pass until it was all *accomplished*. You cannot have some fulfilled, and some not, *without imposing all*. (We will have more to say on the Sabbath issue in another volume).

The seventh day Sabbath foreshadowed the resurrection.

The final three feast days of Israel– the cultic, ceremonial, sacrificial feast days– *likewise foreshadowed the eschatological consummation.*

Those feast days were all *Sabbaths*, just like the seventh day Sabbath.

If the feast day Sabbaths have been annulled, then the seventh day Sabbath has likewise been abrogated.

If those feast days were "fulfilled," which was necessary for them to pass away, then that which the seventh day Sabbath foretold– resurrection and salvation– has likewise been fulfilled.

You cannot divorce the typological meaning of the seventh day Sabbath from the foreshadowing of the feast days. If one Sabbath remains unfulfilled, then all remain unfulfilled– and all remain binding!

Paul's words in Galatians 5 are *apropos* here. In dealing with the Judaizers, who sought to impose Torah, and particularly circumcision, on Christians, Paul said, "I testify to every man that is circumcised, that he is a debtor to do the whole law" (Galatians 5:3). It is either "all in," or "all out." There can be no dichotomization of the law into various elements, some applicable, some passe. It all stands or falls together.

It should finally be noted that the Sabbatarians, and some Dominionists, emphasize that Jesus said, "until heaven and earth passes away, that Torah would not be annulled. We are told that since the literal "heaven and earth" is clearly still here, that Torah must remain valid. The problem here is the assumption that "heaven and earth" must refer to the literal terra firma and the heavens above. But, let me offer a few "bullet points."

As we have seen above, those who maintain the abiding validity of Torah because the literal creation remains, then turn around and tell us that *some of the Law has in fact passed away.* To say the least, this is self-contradictory. You cannot say that not one jot or one tittle shall pass until (literal) heaven and earth passes, and then turn around and say that some of the jots and tittles have passed. That is like saying that some of the heaven and the earth have passed away.

It will be admitted of course, that if Jesus was referring to the literal heaven and earth, then it is *prima facie* evident that none of Torah has passed. But, is it possible that he had something other than the physical cosmos in mind? Go back and read our discussion of the passing of "heaven and earth" to see how this was not only possible, but probable.

My point here, to return to it, is that it is widely recognized that the term "heaven and earth" does not demand that it refers to literal creation.

Fletcher-Lewis, after examining the major Matthean usages of "heaven and earth" made some remarkable and significant remarks about this term as found on the lips of Jesus: "Within the broader sweep of the temple focus throughout this eschatological chapter and the specific time reference of the preceding verse (Mark 13:30; Matthew 24:34), Jesus' promise that 'heaven and earth' will pass away makes best sense, not as a collapse of the space-time universe, as has been so often understood, but as a collapse of a *mythical* space-time universe which is embodied in the Jerusalem temple."[169]

---

[169] Crispin H. T. Fletcher-Louis, "The Destruction of the Temple and the Relativization of the Old Covenant," *Eschatology in the Bible and Theology, Evangelical Essays at the Dawn of a New Millennium*, (Downer's Grove, Ill., InterVarsity, 1997)157. Louis made the comments in regard to Matthew 24:35, but, the comments apply equally to Matthew

I concur, and suggest that this is what Jesus had in mind in Matthew 5. After all, as we have seen, Jesus clearly posits fulfillment of all things that are written" in the context of the demise of the temple.

So, what we are saying is this. Those who claim on the one hand that not one iota of Torah would pass until it was all fulfilled at the end of literal heaven and earth, and who then turn around and say that the sacrifices, the temple cultus, priesthood, physical circumcision, etc. etc., have passed away, are, to say the very least, self contradictory. The problem, part of it, as we have emphasized, is in the identification of "heaven and earth" as *terra firma.*

It is eminently illogical to affirm the passing of any of Torah, while literal creation stands, if Jesus had in mind the material cosmos. On the other hand, the reality that "heaven and earth" was a common Hebraic idiom referring to the Jerusalem temple, brings clear light to what Jesus was saying.

Both the Old Covenant and the New, posit the fulfillment of all things at the time of the judgment of Israel. Thus, Jesus' words were simply echoing what many Jews of the time believed:

"The destruction of the Temple could only mean one thing.... God was inaugurating the promised 'end times', the times when he would finally establish his own true Temple in Jerusalem. As a result, when the disciples asked about the Temple's destruction, they might have been working on the assumption that the calamitous event would mark the inauguration of the long promised 'end times.'"[170]

In other words, destruction of the Temple and the fulfillment of eschatological prophecies were siamese twins that cannot be separated.

5.

[170] P. W. L. Walker, *Jesus and the Holy City*, (Grand Rapids, Eerdmans, 1996)8.

#7 All Does Not Mean All Because...
Related to points # 2 and 4, it is often argued that the prophetic element of the Old Law was not in fact "the law." So, "the law" is dichotomized into "the law" (moral mandates by some, ceremonial commands by others[171]) and then the rest of the prophecies / promises of the Old Testament.

Response:
Terry Benton claims that, "Matthew 5.17f is about all the 'commands' being fulfilled. Jesus did not come to destroy but to fulfill all righteousness... All promises are not under consideration."[172]

Those not familiar with the churches of Christ fellowship cannot fully appreciate how much of a departure from "tradition" Benton's claim truly is. This is a *radical* alteration of the church of Christ traditional definition of "the law."

Let me share with you again the quote from Robert Taylor, who expresses the traditional view of the churches of Christ in regard to the

---

[171] It will be quickly seen that if one calls the "ceremonial laws" concerning the feast days and animal sacrifices "the law" then patently, all that those festal, sacrificial mandates foreshadowed had to be fully accomplished for Torah, any of it, to pass. Realizing this, some now say that *some* of "the law" i.e. the cultic commands were removed, but, the Decalogue– which of course contained the typological Sabbath– remains valid. However, they then say that all of the Decalogue remains valid, *except the Sabbath!* This is the position now taken by Kurt Simmons. See our written debate: *The Passing of Torah: At the Cross or AD 70.* So, once again, this means that *some* of the Law would pass when *some* of it was fulfilled, in direct violation of Jesus' words.

[172] Terry Benton, a church of Christ minister with whom I had a formal written debate, made this claim in a speech in 2011. A PDF of that presentation is found at: http://eciconference.com/page7/assets/02%20The%20Abrogati on%20of%20the%20Law%20-%20Terry%20Benton%20-%2 02011%20ECIC.pdf. My debate with Benton is archived on both my websites.

definition of Torah:: "A devilish device is sometimes resorted to by those who want to keep intact part of the Mosaic System with the remnant abrogated or abolished. They seek to make a distinction between the Law of God and the Law of Moses or between the moral law that God gave and the ceremonial law given by Moses. It all came wrapped up in the same package. It, at times, is called Moses' law; he received it at Sinai. It, at times, is called the Law of God because He gave it at Sinai. The two are used interchangeably"[173]

Okay, so according to Taylor it is "devilish" to dichotomize the Law of Moses into moral commands versus ceremonial law– which, remember, is *prophetic*! But, Benton, seeking to counter Covenant Eschatology takes that "devilish device," and makes it his key argument. Perhaps we need to set up a debate between Benton and Taylor and let them see who is right. One thing is for certain, Benton is far outside the traditional lines of the Restoration Movement leaders.

What Benton and others offering this objection must demonstrate is where, *in the text*, does Jesus make such a delineation? Where does Jesus say, or intimate, that he was speaking of "moral commands" versus promises? In fact, where does he delineate between any kind of commands?[174] As we shall see also, Jesus' use of *genetai* for *fulfill* in v. 18 completely falsifies Benton's claims.

Make no mistake: Benton would affirm the passing of the Sabbath– embedded in the Decalogue. He would say that the ceremonial laws were annulled. But, to say that the ceremonial laws were abrogated *demands total prophetic fulfillment*– i.e. the eschatological consummation found in the last three of Israel's "ceremonial" laws. So, to avoid this conundrum, Benton would be forced to affirm the annulment of those laws / commands without their fulfillment– violating Jesus' words.

Luke 24:44f is a text that is overlooked by those who claim that only the moral commandments of Torah had to be fulfilled. Read Jesus' words:

---

[173] Taylor, in a speech given at a lectureship in Mississippi. (The *Two Covenants*, Pulaski, Tn, Sain Publications, 1996)223.

[174]

142

"Then He said to them, "These are the words which I spoke to you while I was still with you, that all things must be fulfilled which were written in the Law of Moses and the Prophets and the Psalms concerning Me."And He opened their understanding, that they might comprehend the Scriptures. Then He said to them, "Thus it is written, and thus it was necessary for the Christ to suffer and to rise from the dead the third day, and that repentance and remission of sins should be preached in His name to all nations, beginning at Jerusalem." (Luke 24:44-47)

Jesus' words here falsify Benton's claims. Carefully take note: Jesus said that he had taught them that, "all things must be fulfilled which are written in the Law of Moses and the prophets." Where do we find Jesus telling his disciples of the necessity for fulfilling the law and the prophets? Matthew 5:17f comes to mind immediately. So, here in Luke we have Jesus completely destroying the contention that only commandments had to be fulfilled. He specifically says that all things in the law *and the prophets* had to be fulfilled. For Jesus, there was no "commands" versus "promises" as posited by Benton and others.

Jesus did not exclude the prophetic books from that which was necessary to be fulfilled. So, as we shall see immediately below, the fulfillment of prophecy was just as divinely necessary as the fulfillment of commandments. And really, if you stop to think about it, this is the only thing that makes sense in Matthew 5.

Benton says that all that Jesus had to do for Torah to pass was to keep the commandments, not fulfill the promises (prophecies). Well, does Benton believe that Jesus had to fulfill the OT prophecies of his death on the cross for Torah to pass? Make no mistake, *he assuredly does!* But, the predictions of Jesus' death on the cross were not commandments, they were, well, *prophecies and promises*, which Benton assures us did not have to be fulfilled for Torah to pass. The inconsistency here is glaring.

If Jesus had to fulfill even one of the OT prophecies for Torah to pass, *then he had to accomplish all of them*: "Not one jot or one tittle shall pass until it is all accomplished."

In Luke, Jesus not only said that all things written in the law and the prophets had to be fulfilled, he also said this: "Thus it is written and thus it was necessary for the Christ to suffer and to rise from the dead

143

the third day, and that repentance and remission of sins should be preached in His name to all nations beginning at Jerusalem."

Jesus posited the divine necessity for the fulfilling of several things here.

√ His suffering. Let it be carefully noted that Jesus' suffering was not a "command" but a prophecy. See for instance Isaiah 49, 53, etc. So, here is Jesus saying that it was a divine necessity for him to suffer in order to fulfill all things. And remember, Jesus told them, "when I was still with you" he had told them of the necessity to fulfill all things. So, in other words, Jesus said it was divinely necessary to fulfill all things in the law and the prophets. And here in Luke, he tells us it was divinely necessary *to suffer and to die*. Let me re-emphasize here, that these things that had to be fulfilled were not commands. These were prophecies of Messiah's death that had to be fulfilled.

√ Not only was it divinely necessary for Jesus to suffer to fulfill all things, but, it was equally necessary for him to rise from the dead the third day. Those who see the Atonement consummated in the singular action of the cross and Jesus' death are confronted with a severe problem here. The resurrection of Christ was ever bit as much of a divine necessity, as an integral element of the Atonement process, as was his death on the cross. Of course, this agrees perfectly with the type / anti-type praxis of the Old Covenant Day of Atonement as outlined in Hebrews 9-10.

There is no way to outline what Jesus said in the following manner: It was divinely necessary to fulfill the OT prophecies of his suffering in order for Torah to pass. However, it was not divinely necessary for him to rise from the dead for the Law to pass. Such a structuring of what Jesus said does great violence to the text. His resurrection, to reiterate, was as divinely necessary for the fulfilling of all things, the things in the law and prophets, as was his death on the cross.

At the risk of redundancy, let it be noted again that the prophecies of Jesus' resurrection were just that– prophecies and promises. They were not commands for him to fulfill. And yet, Jesus said that when he was with them he had told them he had to fulfill all things in the law *and the prophets*, and now, he carefully shows that those prophecies that

144

had to be fulfilled included his resurrection– which extends beyond the cross.

By the way, where do we find the prophecy or prophecies of Jesus' resurrection on the third day? Most scholars believe that this is a referent, an echo if you will, of Hosea 6:1-3. And if so, that brings us to the realization– the indisputable fact– that Jesus was saying that until all prophecy was fulfilled, none of Torah would pass. Remember, when he was still with them, he had told the disciples that "all things in the law and the prophets" had to be fulfilled. Now, he shows that this included his resurrection. This means that if any prophecy had to be fulfilled for Torah to pass, then all prophecy had to pass– not simply the prophecy of his death. But there is even more.

√ Jesus now expands the list of items that were necessary in order to fulfill "all things" in the law and the prophets: ...and that, repentance and remission of sins should be preached in His name to all nations, beginning at Jerusalem" (Luke 24. 47).

Jesus' use of the conjunction in the "and that" links the necessity for his passion to the preaching of the gospel to all the nations on an equal footing. Thus, not only was Jesus' death and resurrection divinely necessary for the fulfillment of all things written in the law and the prophets, the completion of the world mission was equally, divinely necessary. So, once again, the claim that all Jesus had to do to fulfill all things was for him to personally fulfill the commandments is falsified by Jesus' words.

Here, Jesus shows that the fulfillment of all things in the law and the prophets included the fulfillment of the World Mission, which of course, was from the Old Covenant prophets.

Isaiah 11 foretold that in the day of Messiah, when he would be raised as a banner to the people, "the earth shall be full of the knowledge of the Lord" (Isaiah 11.9; see also Habakkuk 2:19).

Notice that in Isaiah, we find the lifting up of Messiah, which is probably a referent to his death (John 12:32). Thus, here is one of those "promises" that Jesus had to fulfill for Torah to pass. But, of course, Isaiah links the lifting up of Messiah with the proclamation of the gospel of that Messiah!

So, we have indisputable evidence and Biblical testimony– the words of Jesus himself, that it was necessary for the gospel to be preached into all the world in order to fulfill all things that are in the law and the prophets.

Note carefully Jesus' words: "Do not think that I am come to destroy the law and the prophets. I did not come to destroy, but to fulfill." What Benton and others fail to acknowledge is that this is an elliptical statement. In other words, when Jesus said "but to fulfill" it is a direct referent back to "the law and the prophets."

It is grammatically untenable to say that Jesus was saying that he came to fulfill simply "the law." His words demand that "but to fulfill" are inclusive of "the law and the prophets." And that being true, the attempt by all futurists to divide Torah up into moral law versus ceremonial law, versus prophecy, are invalidated and falsified.

Benton also overlooks the fact that Torah was full of ceremonial and cultic *commands*.[175] In fact, the entire festal calendar was a long list of such commands to offer sacrifice. And what cannot be ignored is how foundational those festal events were to Israel's eschatological hope and expectation, as we have seen. The point is that Benton's claim has no merit, either from the immediate context of Matthew 5 where there is no delineation between what had to be fulfilled (moral commands) and what did not (prophecies). His claim is nothing but a fabricated theory to avoid the power of Jesus' language.

Finally, Benton clearly does not see the implication of what he has said. He claims that all that Jesus had to fulfill were the moral commands. But remember, Jesus is talking about what would pass when it was fulfilled. In other words, what was to be fulfilled is what was to pass.

So, per Benton's "logic" when Jesus completely fulfilled the moral commands, *it is the moral commands that passed away!* You cannot define "the law" as the moral commands which were the focus of

---

[175] Perhaps Benton would counter that those cultic commands were not "moral commands." Once again the burden of proof would lie with him to demonstrate that distinction in Matthew 5, and he patently cannot do it. Would Benton argue that it was not "immoral" to violate some, any of God's commandments? Where would be the justification for saying that violation of some of God's commandments would be immoral, while the violation of others would not be immoral?

"until all is fulfilled" without thereby affirming that *when Jesus had fulfilled the moral commands that the moral commands passed away.*

Benton would argue, however, that when Jesus fulfilled the moral commandments, that the ceremonial laws and praxis were abrogated. This would mean that Jesus was saying, "When I fulfill one part of the law, the moral commandments, another part of the law, that *is not fulfilled*, will pass away, and the part that I do fulfill will not pass away." Of course, one would never get that message from Jesus' actual words. That concept has to be imported into the text.

I noted earlier how things are changing in the amillennial world, and specifically in the churches of Christ. Benton would *never* make his argument in a debate with a Sabbatarian. And I can assure the reader that those well informed of the history of doctrine in that organization know full well that this is true.

Notice the comment of J. W. McGarvey, one of the most highly regarded scholars of the Campbell- Stone Movement of which Benton is a member.

McGarvey wrote in the *Fourfold Gospel Commentary* that, "the only way to destroy (the law and the prophets) would be to prevent the fulfillment of the predictions contained in them." He continued: "Jesus came to fulfill all the types of the former, and (eventually) all the unfulfilled predictions of the latter. He fulfills them partly in his own person, and partly by his administration of the affairs of the kingdom. The latter part of the process is still going on, and will be until the end of the world."

To say that McGarvey contradicted the text of Matthew 5 is an understatement. He claimed that Torah, all of it, passed at the cross, but here he affirmed *the present application and fulfillment of the law* in the administration of the kingdom continuing until "the end of the world." Thus, per McGarvey's claims, Torah could not have passed, any of it!

See also McGarvey's comments on Acts 3:19f, where he says that the restoration of all things means, "to finally restore that moral sway which God originally exercised over the whole earth. It is doubtless this thought which suggested the term restoration, though reference is had to the fulfillment of all the prophecies which are to be fulfilled on

147

earth.[176] Not till all are fulfilled will Christ come again."[177] Very clearly, McGarvey posited the complete fulfillment of the Old Testament at the end of time. All the while affirming that Jesus removed Torah at the cross!

Bruce likewise notes on Acts 3 that, *"apokatastasis* may here be rendered 'establishment', or 'fulfillment', referring to the fulfillment of all OT prophecy, culminating in the establishment of God's kingdom on earth."[178]

Rackham noted, "The Exodus was completed by the entrance upon Israel's inheritance of Canaan. The loss of that inheritance in the Captivity had deeply impressed on the Jews the idea of Restoration. Restoration became the necessary fulfillment of their recreation, as the Exodus had been the work of Moses, the restoration was assigned to Elijah. As interpreted by the prophets, e.g. Malachi 4:6, the restoration was a moral one, and in that sense John the Baptist had fulfilled Elijah's office. But the idea had received a wider expansion. The restoration which would follow the recreation of Israel had become *the restoration of all things*, both of the world of men and of nature. So Paul taught that the recovery of Israel would be the salvation of the world; and that the creation also would share in the liberty of the glory of the children of God. The restoration then was the fulfillment of Isaiah's prediction, of a new heaven and a new earth. But apart from this literal prediction, all the holy prophets which have been since the

---

[176] McGarvey's comments here are a cause of consternation to those in the churches of Christ / Restoration Movement. McGarvey is one of the most revered early scholars of that movement. Yet, he clearly expressed a *postmillennial* eschatological view in Acts 3, which is at odds with the amillennial view that came to characterize the churches of Christ / Christian church movement. The historical reality is that the Restoration leaders were unsettled in their eschatology. There was no consensus of doctrine among them until the twentieth century.

[177] J. W. McGarvey, *Commentary on Acts*, Revised, seventh edition, (Nashville, Tn., Gospel Advocate)58-59.

[178] F. F. Bruce, *Acts with the Greek Text and Commentary*, (Grand Rapids, Eerdmans, 1984)112.

world began, i.e. the whole OT from Genesis 3:15 to Malachi 4:6, had looked forward to a restoration."[179]

Gareth Reese, admitted that Peter was concerned with the fulfillment of OT prophecies made to Israel: "Peter goes on to explain that he is speaking of the fulfillment of the Old Testament prophecies. Peter seems to be saying, 'Jesus will remain in heaven until all things that prophets predicted are fulfilled."[180]

While all of these commentators correctly note that Peter posited the eschatological consummation at the time of the fulfillment of the Old Covenant promises made to Israel, what they all fail to consider is that the "New Moons, Feast Days and Sabbaths" of Torah were all, indisputably, "the law", but, they were likewise prophecy.

Thus, to maintain, as for instance McGarvey did, that prophecy would remain intact "until the end of the world," is to tacitly affirm the abiding validity of all of Torah, because *the prophecies of the eschatological consummation are inseparable from "the law."*

The eschatological consummation is when Israel's prophecies would be fulfilled. The parousia, judgment and resurrection would only come when Israel's festal calendar, i.e. the final three feast days of Rosh Ha Shanah (Feast of Trumpets), Final Atonement, and Succot (Feast of Harvest) would be fully accomplished. All that they foretold, judgment, salvation and resurrection would finally be brought to pass.[181]

Likewise, to reiterate, those cultic, sacrificial feast days were undeniably part of "the law." Thus, to affirm that Christ will not return until, "all of the prophecies that are to be fulfilled on the earth are fulfilled" is to say that not one jot or one tittle of Israel's cultic world,

---

[179] Richard Rackham, *Acts of the Apostles,* (London, Methuen and Co., 1947)53.

[180] Gareth Reese, *New Testament History, Acts* (Joplin, College Press, 1983)166.

[181] It is our plan to devote one volume in this series to an examination of the Festal Calendar of Israel and the passing of Torah. This is one of the most ignored themes in the entire discussion.

all sacrifices, all feast days, all pilgrimages, remain valid and mandatory. This is inescapable.

What we have seen then, in response to the objection, is that there simply is no justification, no evidence, to support the idea that all Jesus had to do was fulfill the moral commands of Torah for the law to pass.

Jesus' words stand as a powerful refutation of all attempts by futurists to have Torah pass away without the total, complete fulfillment of all things found therein. Jesus said that not one iota of the smallest detail of the law would pass until it was all fully accomplished. The great question is therefore, where does scripture posit the fulfillment of all things.

Well, we have actually answered that question somewhat above, but, I want now to examine several texts that identify the time when "all things that are written must be fulfilled."

WHEN WERE ALL THINGS FULFILLED– THE BIBLICAL TESTIMONY

Daniel 9.24-27
"Seventy weeks are determined… to seal vision and prophecy"

In my book *Seal Up Vision and Prophecy* I give a substantial body of proof from scholars across the entire spectrum of eschatological belief to the effect that the term seal vision and prophecy entails the cessation of the prophetic office *due to the fulfillment of all prophecy.*[182]

Thus, Daniel's prophecy posited the fulfillment of all prophecy by the end of the 70 week period. And the thing is that one cannot, in spite of the dispensational claims to the contrary, extend the seventy weeks beyond the fall of Jerusalem in AD 70.

Remember the objection that says Christ removed the law, but that prophecy remains valid? Well, Daniel 9.24-27 negates the force of that argument.

When Daniel was told that 70 weeks were determined to seal vision and prophecy, the angel did not say, "70 weeks are determined to seal *the* vision and *the* prophecy" thereby indicating that only the 70 week prophecy was in view. But, t*here is no definite article in the text of Daniel 9:24.* This indicates, as numerous scholars have noted, that "To seal vision and prophet" designates that the object of the expression is to be taken in a broad, universal sense.[183] In other words, Daniel was not being told that 70 weeks were determined to fulfill "*the* prophecy" i.e. the prophecy of Daniel 9 alone.[184]

---

[182] Don K. Preston *Seal Up Vision and Prophecy* (Ardmore, Ok. JaDon Management, 2007). Available from my websites, Amazon, and other retailers.

[183] E. W. Hengstenberg, *Christology of The Old Testament*, (Grand Rapids, Kregel, 1970)409.

[184] In my 2004 debate with amillennialist Thomas Thrasher, my arguments on Daniel 9 had a visible impact on Thrasher. I noted the absence of the definite article, to which he then– incredibly– claimed that there is a definite article in the text! He was so desperate to offset the force of the

Lange stated that since the article is missing the reference is evidently, "Not to any particular prophet or prophecy, but rather to the prophetic institution and its visions relative to the prospective salvation in general. The idea is, that everything in the form of prophetic visions and predictions that had been produced in the course of theocratic development from the time of Moses...should receive 'sealing' I. e. Divine confirmation and recognition in the form of actual fulfillment."[185] (Lange, 1876,195).

Here is the point: Even if one were to admit that Torah ended at the cross (which of course I do not admit), the objection that Torah passed but prophecy continued still leads to the full preterist paradigm since *Daniel posits the fulfillment of all prophecy no later than AD 70.*

Please note the difficulty that Daniel 9 presents for amillennialism and postmillennialism to a degree.

Amillennialists, as we have seen, affirm that God was through with Israel at the cross, although an increasing number are admitting that it was in AD 70. Postmillennialists commonly say that the Law of Moses ended in the first century, in AD 70 (e.g. DeMar, Gentry, etc.).

For instance, as we have seen, Joel McDurmon says that the Law of Moses "died in AD 70."[186] Well, if the Law of Moses ended in AD 70,

---

argument that he was willing to make an argument on the italicized, i.e *the supplied*, article! I responded by noting his desperation and then observed that even if one admitted that the focus of seal vision and prophecy was solely Daniel 9, that this did not help his case because Daniel 9 predicted the resurrection of the dead! Thus, even if it is granted (which is false) that the angel was saying that 70 weeks were determined for the fulfillment of Daniel 9, then since Daniel 9 foretold the resurrection, this demands the fulfillment of the resurrection no later than AD 70– where Thrasher posits the end of the 70 weeks! Thrasher had no response for this. Audios of that debate are available from me.

[185] John Peter Lange, *Commentary on the Holy Scriptures, Ezekiel-Daniel*, edited by Phillip Schaff, (Grand Rapids, Zondervan, 1876)195.

[186] Joel McDurmon, *Jesus v Jerusalem* (Powder Springs, GA, American Vision, 2011)47. McDurmon's book

then God's covenant with Israel, her covenant history, ended there. This means that all of God's Old Covenant eschatological promises were fulfilled at that juncture. There are no eschatological promises separate and apart from God's Old Covenant promises made to Israel.

Here is my point: Daniel 9 is about "your people and your city" i.e. the prophecy deals with Israel and her covenant history. It is not about the church divorced from Israel. It is not about the end of the Christian age. It is not about the end of history.

What is so critical about this point is that the six constituent elements listed in Daniel 9:24 are undeniably eschatological elements. They are, to be more specific, tied to the resurrection.[187] Let me briefly elucidate.

The putting away of sin is clearly eschatological and soteriological (Hebrews 9:26-28). Paul posits the final victory over sin for those in Christ at the resurrection, when sin, "the sting of death" would be overcome. And what cannot be missed is that Paul likewise posits that final victory at the accomplishment (*genetai*) of God's Old Covenant promises made to Israel– just like Daniel says.

Now, virtually everyone admits that the resurrection is when all prophecy is fulfilled. With that in mind, notice my argument stated here in simplified form for ease of understanding:

The time of the resurrection is the time of the final fulfillment of all prophecy.

The time of the resurrection is the time of the final victory over sin, the sting of death (1 Corinthians 15:55-56).

But, the time of the "putting away of sin" is an Old Covenant promise, confined to the seventy weeks of Daniel 9:24.

---

is, in many ways, *outstanding*, but illustrates the inherent contradictions in the postmillennial world. The book is available from my websites: www.eschatology.org, or www.bibleprophecy.com.

[187] See my *Seventy Weeks Are Determined... For the Resurrection* for a full development of this critical claim.

Therefore, the final fulfillment of all prophecy– the time of the final victory over sin– is confined to the seventy weeks of Daniel 9:24.

The identical argument can be made concerning the making of Atonement, the bringing in of everlasting righteousness and the anointing of the Most Holy. These are all eschatological tenets and motifs, inseparably connected to the resurrection. So, to reiterate, where ever one posits the consummation of Israel's covenant history, it is there that the resurrection– the fulfillment of all prophecy– takes place. But, to re-emphasize, you cannot extend the seventy weeks of Daniel 9 beyond the AD 70 fall of Jerusalem.

So, Daniel foretold the resurrection. The resurrection is the time of the complete fulfillment of all prophecy. Daniel's prophecy concerned the end of Israel's covenant age, and the fulfillment of God's promises to her. Daniel 9 is not, repeat, not a prophecy of the end of the Christian age. It is not about the end of time. It is not about the church divorced from Israel and her promises. But, Daniel's prophecy extends no further than the fall of Jerusalem in AD 70– the overwhelming flood, the end of the seventy weeks. Therefore, the fulfillment of all prophecy occurred no later than the fall of Jerusalem in AD 70. And this agrees perfectly with Jesus' words in Luke 21.22.

Luke 21:22
We will defer our comments on Luke 21:22 for now and reserve them for our response to Kenneth Gentry that will follow this section. Will only make a brief observation.

As he described and predicted the AD 70 catastrophe coming on Jerusalem, Jesus said: "These be the days of vengeance in which all things that are written must be fulfilled."

Notice the perfect harmony between Luke 21 and Daniel 9. Daniel was told that seventy weeks were determined to fulfill all prophecy, and the terminus of his vision was the AD 70 destruction of Jerusalem

154

(v. 26-27).[188] Jesus predicted (reiterated Daniel) that same judgment, and said that when it came all things that are written must be fulfilled.

Acts 3:21-24

Peter, speaking of Jesus as Messiah, said:

"Whom heaven must receive until the times of restoration of all things, which God has spoken by the mouth of all His holy prophets since the world began. For Moses truly said to the fathers, 'The LORD your God will raise up for you a Prophet like me from your brethren. Him you shall hear in all things, whatever He says to you. And it shall be that every soul who will not hear that Prophet shall be utterly destroyed from among the people.'Yes, and all the prophets, from Samuel and those who follow, as many as have spoken, have also foretold these days."

While there are several things that could be noted, let me enumerate some of the more salient issues that bear on our discussion.

☛ Christ would remain in heaven "until the restoration of all things." As I note in my *We Shall Meet Him In The Air*,[189] the work of the restoration was initiated by John as Elijah (Matthew 17:10-12). This fact is recognized among many postmillennialists.

Mathison for instance, commenting on Matthew 9:18-34 and Jesus' healing of numerous individuals, says this was the fulfillment of Isaiah 35:5-6. He says, "His healing of the blind and the mute indicates that the prophesied time of the eschatological restoration has arrived (Isaiah 35:5-6)" (2009, 357).

---

[188] Postmillennialists claim that the destruction of Jerusalem was actually outside the seventy week countdown. They tell us that the destruction was "determined" within the seventy weeks, but fulfilled afterward. See my *Seal Up Vision and Prophecy* for a refutation of this position. The book is available from my websites, Amazon and other retailers.

[189] Don K. Preston, *We Shall Meet Him In The Air, the Wedding of the King of kings.* (Ardmore, Ok. 73401, JaDon Management Inc., 2010)255+.

If, as Mathison, Gentry and others affirm, the restoration had begun, this means that Christ's parousia was to *consummate* what had already begun by John.

☞ That restoration was foretold by, "all His holy prophets since the world began." Thus, this firmly establishes Peter's eschatology– just as Paul's-- as the hope of Israel found in the OT. Peter did not have an eschatology divorced from Israel and the OT prophets. He did not have a New Testament eschatology opposed to Old Testament eschatology.[190]

☞Note that Peter cites Deuteronomy 18 and Moses' prediction of the coming of the prophet like Moses. What is to be noted is that according to Peter, obedience to Jesus was equal to the obedience to Moses.

Furthermore, it is to be noted that rejection of Jesus would result in being utterly cut off "out from" (from "*ek*" meaning out from) among the people" (Acts 3:23). Peter was threatening his audience with Covenantal Wrath– Mosaic Covenant Wrath.[191]

☞ Peter is emphatic in telling his audience that all of those OT prophets – all who had ever spoken– "foretold these days" (Acts 3.24). Peter was not, as demanded by the millennial paradigm, saying that

---

[190] Postmillennialists, like amillennialists, insist on an Edenic Eschatology as opposed to a "Jewish" eschatology. In my debate with postmillennialist James Jordan he repeatedly claimed that the eschatology of Genesis was not the eschatology of AD 70. In response, I noted that all the NT writers subsumed the Edenic eschatology into the story of Israel, to be fulfilled at the end of her covenant age. My debate with Jordan is now available from me in book form, on Amazon and from other retailers.

[191] In another volume in this series, we will demonstrate the critical role of John the Baptizer as the covenant messenger to warn Israel of coming wrath. John heralded that impending judgment, and now, Peter is reiterating those warnings. Since that message was impending application of the Mosaic Covenant Wrath it is obvious that Torah did not pass at the Cross.

those OT prophets foretold a time far removed from his first century generation.

Jesus said the OT worthies and prophets longed to see the fulfillment of their prophecies but did not see it. However, he said that his first century audience, his apostles and disciples, were in fact witnessing the fulfillment of those promises in Torah (Matthew 13:17f).

Likewise, Peter later wrote that the OT prophets did not know the exact nature or time for the fulfillment of their prophecies, except, they were told that fulfillment was not for their days. The apostle said, however, that: "all the prophets, from Samuel and those who follow, as many as have spoken, have also foretold these days" (Acts 3:24).

Jesus _came_ (Incarnation) to fulfill– but not all things.

He was _coming_ (parousia) to fulfill– all things (Acts 3)

Jesus' incarnation continued the "restoration of all things" initiated by John.

The parousia would consummate the fulfillment.

Peter said every prophet who had ever written of the consummation wrote of "these days" his first century generation.

Thus, all prophecy was to be fulfilled in Peter's generation.

So, Peter tells us that the OT prophets foretold the restoration of all things at the parousia of Christ, when all prophecy would be accomplished, and he said that all of those OT prophets foretold his first century generation. This agrees perfectly with Daniel 9 and Luke 21:22.

What we have then is this. Jesus said he came to fulfill, and, he was coming to fulfill all things! Thus, those who claim that Jesus' incarnation is all that was necessary to "fulfill all things" are clearly not considering all of the Biblical testimony.

157

1 Corinthians 15:54f

"So when this corruptible has put on incorruption, and this mortal has put on immortality, then shall be brought to pass the saying that is written: "Death is swallowed up in victory." "O Death, where is your sting? O Hades, where is your victory?" The sting of death is sin, and the strength of sin is the law."

Admittedly, this text does not specifically mention the fulfillment of all prophecy. However, virtually everyone agrees that the time of the resurrection is the end of the age. It is the time of Christ's coming. It is the "end of all things": "then comes the end, when he shall deliver the kingdom to the Father" (1 Corinthians 15:24). In other words, the resurrection is when all prophecy would be fulfilled.

With this in mind, let's go back to Matthew 5:17-18 where Jesus said "I did not come to destroy, but to fulfill, for verily I say until you that not one jot or one tittle shall pass from the law until it is all *fulfilled.*

We have already noted Jesus' use of two distinct words. He used *pleroma*" in his first use of "fulfill." However, in v. 18, when he said "until it is all fulfilled" he uses another word, which brings greater clarity and power to the discussion. That word, as noted briefly above, is *genetai. (Genetai* is a third person, singular, aorist (2) subjunctive of *genomai*).

It is worth noting that *genetai* means "to bring to pass, to accomplish.." Nolland struggles with Matthew 5:17-18[192] but on *genetai* says, "The clause remains difficult, but it seems most likely to be concerned to guarantee a permanence to the Law until such time as every item on the Law's agenda has been achieved. Until all that it lays out as God's will for humankind has been accomplished."[193] Hagner

---

[192] Part of the reason for Nolland's struggles is that he takes the referent to "heaven and earth" to mean the literal creation. I suggest that this is untenable in the light of what Jesus is saying in the text. He clearly foresaw the passing of Torah at the full realization of what Torah foretold– the New Covenant world of Messiah.

[193] John Nolland, *New International Greek Testament Commentary*, Matthew, (Eerdmans, Grand Rapids, Paternoster, 2005)221.

concurs that *genetai* means "until it is all accomplished", "until it has all occurred."[194] Hendrickson says, "the meaning, then, is this, that not even in the slightest respect will the Old Testament remain unfulfilled."[195]

Nolland and Hagner catch the meaning of *genetai* very well, and an examination of some other texts in which the word appears confirms this meaning of "fully accomplish." But, first, let me note how *genetai* falsifies one of the objections that is offered to counter the force of Matthew 5.

In my formal written debate with Jerry McDonald, he said that Matthew 5:18 does not demand complete fulfillment of all of Torah. He said that Jesus simply "set in motion" the fulfillment process and that this is all that was necessary for Torah to pass. Unfortunately for McDonald and those who hold to this somewhat desperate position, the reality of Jesus' incarnation falsifies this claim.

The cross was simply not the event that "set in motion" the process of fulfillment. As Hendrickson succinctly notes, "As Jesus was speaking, some parts of the Old Testament had already been fulfilled, for example, the incarnation. Other parts were being fulfilled. Still others were to be fulfilled soon, that is, the crucifixion and the resurrection; or were to be fulfilled later, in the ascension, at and after Pentecost, and finally at Christ's return in glory" (2002, 291). Now, it is clear that Hendrickson does not see the implication of his own statements in regard to the passing of Torah. Nonetheless, he is clearly correct to note that *the cross was not the initiation of a process of fulfillment.* That process of fulfillment began well before the cross.

Note again that *genetai* means to fully accomplish, to bring to reality. Then, note Jesus' actual words "not one jot or one tittle shall pass from the law until it is fully accomplished." So, Jesus did not say that all that was necessary for Torah to pass was for him to "set in motion" the fulfillment process. He said that none of Torah would pass until it was *all* fully accomplished. To say that all that was necessary for Torah to pass was for the process of fulfillment to begin is to say that only part

---

[194] Donald Hagner, *Word Biblical Commentary, Matthew 1-13,* Vol. 33a, (Dallas, Word Publishers, 1993)108.

[195] William Hendrickson, *New International Commentary, Matthew*, (Grand Rapids, Baker, 2002)291.

had to be fully accomplished. This violates Jesus' words that until _all_ was _fully accomplished_ none would pass.

If all that was necessary for Torah to pass away was for the process of fulfillment to be set in motion then one could argue that Torah passed away at the appearance of John the Baptizer, since, "the law and the prophets were until John." The "process of fulfillment" of the last days prophecies began with John, thus, Torah should have passed at that point. The "process of fulfillment" was in place well before the cross.

As the old saying goes, "what proves too much, proves nothing." Jesus did not say the law would pass when he had "set in motion" the process of fulfillment. _Genetai_ demands the "full accomplishment" of Torah.

With this in mind, take note now of some of the texts in which _genetai_ occurs.

☛Matthew 24:34-- Jesus predicted his parousia at the end of the age, and assured his disciples: "This generation shall be no means pass until all of these things are fulfilled (_genetai_).

☛1 Corinthians 15:54– As Paul discussed the resurrection, he said "when moral has put on immortality... then shall be shall be brought to pass (_genetai_) the saying..." and he quotes from Isaiah 25:8 and Hosea 13:14. So, the time of the resurrection is when the prophecies Isaiah and Hosea would be "fully accomplished" brought to a reality. More on 1 Corinthians 15 momentarily.

☛ 2 Timothy 2:18– Hymenaeus and Philetus were claiming that the resurrection is already past. They believed it had already been accomplished.[196]

---

[196] See my "The Hymenaean Heresy: Reverse the Charges," MP3 series. To my knowledge it is the most in-depth analysis of 2 Timothy 2, as a preterist response to the charge of heresy, that has been produced. Available on both of my websites: www.eschatology.org and www.bibleprophecy.com.

☛Revelation 1:1– John was informed by Jesus, who was informed by the Father, that, "these things must shortly come to pass" (genetai).

☛Revelation 12:10– With the initial defeat of Satan, the heavenly song was sang: "now is come" (from genetai) salvation , and strength, and the kingdom of our God, and the power of his Christ."

☛Revelation 22:6– At the close of the book, John is reminded of the faithfulness of the God of the prophets, and told once again: "These things must shortly be done."

From this brief survey, it is clear that *genetai* means to accomplish, to bring to reality. Notice then our argument in regard to the resurrection (1 Corinthians 15:54) and Paul's use of *genetai.*

The resurrection, (at the end of the millennium) is when all prophecy would be (will be) completely fulfilled (*genetai*, 1 Corinthians 15:54- This is all but universally agreed).

The resurrection was an integral part of "the law" (the Law of Moses) being foreshadowed in her feast days, and foretold in the prophets, where were themselves "the law."

Not one iota of Torah, the Law of Moses, would pass until it was all fully accomplished (genetai).

Therefore, not one iota of Torah, the Law of Moses, would (will) pass until the full accomplishment of the resurrection promises found in and that were an integral part of the Law of Moses.

Now, with this in mind, let me remind the reader of the all but universally held view that the Law of Moses passed away in the first century. This is the amillennial position, the dispensational view and the postmillennial view as well.[197] But, if the Law has passed, then all

---

[197]   Postmillennialist Joel McDurmon, (Head of Research of American Vision) with whom I had a formal two day debate in July 2012, says the Law of Moses passed away

that the Law anticipated, foreshadowed and foretold has been "fully accomplished." This is what Jesus demanded in Matthew 5:17-18.

It is impossible to over-emphasize this dilemma. While attempts are made to parse Jesus' words into meaning something totally different from what they seem to say, there really is no exegetical, grammatical, or contextual justification for denying the force of what he said.

Thus, when men say that "all" in Jesus' declaration actually meant *some*, I think Bahnsen's words are not only accurate, but *apropos*:

"In Matthew 5:18 the commencement of the law's passing away is made dependent upon *panta genetai*. Panta, when used without an article or preposition indicates "all things, everything" (as in Matthew 11:27; John 1:3; 3:35; 21:17; 1 Corinthians 2:10; 15:27, 28; Ephesians 1:22a; Revelation 21:5); it is to be taken in this absolutely general sense unless the context dictates some antecedent whole of which *panta* constitutes the complete parts" (Bahnsen, *Theonomy*, 2002, 83).[198]

In other words, all means all, unless context demands a particularized application, and clearly, in Matthew 5 there is no specificity applied to "all" (*panta*).

So, when we acknowledge the comprehensive nature of "all" (*panta*) and couple that with *genetai* it is *prima facie* demonstration that until all of Torah– including the prophetic festal calendar,, the Sabbaths, etc.- were all fully accomplished not one iota of Torah would cease to be valid.

Jesus' use of *genetai* in Matthew 5:17-18, coupled with the universal acknowledgment that the resurrection is when all would be *genetai*,

---

in AD 70. (Joel McDurmon, *Jesus V Jerusalem*, (Powder Springs, GA. American Vision, 2011)47. That debate will be, Lord willing, available in printed form in the near future.

[198] While Bahnsen's linguistic analysis is spot on, his theological views are clearly at odds with what he wrote. On the one hand he said that not the slightest particular of the Law would pass until it was all fully accomplished. But then, he affirmed, as we have seen, the passing of the Sabbath, circumcision, the festal calendar and a great host of the minutia of Torah! Of course, Bahnsen is not alone in his inconsistency in this regard.

serves as a serious blow to all futurist eschatologies. They tell us on the one that Torah has passed. Then, they turn around and say that the prophecies found in Torah have not been accomplished. This is specious and untenable.

Revelation 10-11

"The angel whom I saw standing on the sea and on the land raised up his hand to heaven and swore by Him who lives forever and ever, who created heaven and the things that are in it, the earth and the things that are in it, and the sea and the things that are in it, that there should be delay no longer, but in the days of the sounding of the seventh angel, when he is about to sound, the mystery of God would be finished, as He declared to His servants the prophets" (Revelation 10:5-7).

"Then the seventh angel sounded: And there were loud voices in heaven, saying, "The kingdoms of this world have become the kingdoms of our Lord and of His Christ, and He shall reign forever and ever!" 16 And the twenty-four elders who sat before God on their thrones fell on their faces and worshiped God, saying: "We give You thanks, O Lord God Almighty, The One who is and who was and who is to come, Because You have taken Your great power and reigned. The nations were angry, and Your wrath has come, And the time of the dead, that they should be judged, And that You should reward Your servants the prophets and the saints, And those who fear Your name, small and great, And should destroy those who destroy the earth."

Note that chapter 10 posits the fulfillment of all that the prophets foretold at the sounding of the seventh trump. Then notice that in chapter 11 the sounding of the seventh trump is the time of the resurrection and the rewarding of the dead.

So, once again, we find the time of the resurrection posited as the time of the fulfillment of all prophecy.

Of course, what should not be missed is the direct connection between Revelation 10-11 and Daniel 9 and Daniel 12.

I will give here an edited and revised excerpt from my book *Who Is This Babylon* that demonstrates the parallels and sets the proper context.

Daniel foresaw the time of the end and the resurrection (Daniel 12:2-4). The prophet sees and hears one angel ask another angel, "How long shall the fulfillment of these wonders be?" (Daniel 12:6). Very clearly, Revelation 10: 5-6 is a direct echo of Daniel 12:6.

In response to the angel's question, heaven responds about when the vision will be fulfilled! The responding angel, "held up his right hand to heaven, and swore by Him who lives for ever and ever, that it shall be a time, times and half a time." (Daniel 12:7).

Now, unless there are two different "time, times and half a time" periods for the consummation of Biblical eschatology, then this means that Daniel 12 ties in directly with the earlier prophecy of the little horn prophecy of Daniel 7, the persecution of the saints by the beast in Revelation, the testimony of the two witnesses and the fate of the two cities in Revelation, i.e. the holy city and the harlot city. Since it is agreed by virtually all commentators that all of these referents are to the same time, i.e. the time of the end,[199] then this much should be clear:

First, we are dealing with the same time period as Daniel 9, i.e. the fulfillment of the Seventy Weeks, since Daniel 9 and Daniel 12 both deal with the fate of Daniel's people (Daniel 9:24; Daniel 12:1). Thus, all of these referents must be viewed within the confines of God's dealings with Israel. If in fact Daniel 9 and Daniel 12 are dealing with the same time subject, then there is simply no way to posit either text into a far distant future and "end of time" application.

Second, if Daniel 9 and Daniel 12 are parallel texts, then since the seventy weeks of Daniel 9 consummate in the "overwhelming flood" of the time of the end against "your people and your holy city" (Daniel

---

[199] Some commentators, especially amillennialists, believe that Daniel 7 and Revelation deal with the rise and ascendency of the Roman Catholic church. Yet, even in this view, it is held that the papacy is destroyed at the time of the end. Wayne Jackson in the June, 1993 issue of the *Christian Courier*, attempted to make the case for applying Daniel 7 to the Papacy. You can read my response on my website: www.eschatology.org.

164

9:24), then this means that Daniel 12 must consummate at that same time.

Third, if Daniel 9 and Daniel 12 are parallel, then since the "time, times and half a time" of Daniel 12 are also the ground for Revelation 11-13, then this means that the "time, times and half a time" of Revelation is inextricably bound up with the fulfillment of the seventy weeks and the fate of "your people and your holy city." The implications for our understanding of Revelation are profound once we acknowledge this context.

Of course, our millennial friends gladly agree that Daniel 9 and Revelation deal with the fate of Israel. The unfortunate thing is that they posit that fulfillment into the future, after an imagined rapture, and fail to see that the New Testament writers were anticipating the fulfillment of Daniel and even Revelation in their lifetime.

Wuest revealed this mentality in an article, "The Rapture–Precisely When?" Commenting on Revelation 1:19, and the fact that John was told to write of things, "that shall be hereafter," Wuest notes the use of the Greek word *mello* with the infinitive, "The Greek of 'shall be' is not the verb of being in the future tense, but the verb *mello* is used with an infinitive. It is a device the Greek writer uses when he wishes to indicate that a thing predicted will come to pass very soon, an idea that the simple future does not carry."[200]

So, John uses *mello* with the infinitive to "indicate that a thing predicted will come to pass very soon." Yet, Wuest, and all millennialists, believes that it has now been 2000 years since John wrote of the things that must come to pass very soon! There can be no doubt that John anticipated the fulfillment of Daniel and of his Apocalypse, "very soon." And he was not disappointed!

Fourth, Daniel not only heard that the end time events would be fulfilled at the end of "the time, times and half a time," but heaven then answered the question so definitively that there can be no escape. The time, times and half a time would be consummated, "when the power

---

[200] Kenneth Wuest, Litt.D, "The Rapture–Precisely When?," Midnight Call Magazine, October, 2005, p. 3. The article can be found at:
http://www.midnightcall.com/pdf/em0510.pdf

of the holy people has been completely shattered, all of these things will be fulfilled" (Daniel 12:7b).

So, Daniel's seventy weeks would be fulfilled, "when the power of the holy people has been completely shattered," and this agrees perfectly with his prediction that "the end thereof shall be with a flood" when "the holy city" would suffer desolation (Daniel 9:27).

Further, "the time, times and half a time"would be fulfilled when the city that killed the two witnesses, and was, "where the Lord was slain," was destroyed (Revelation 11:6-8). This agrees perfectly with Daniel's prediction that the time of the end would be, "when the power of the holy people has been completely shattered, all of these things will be fulfilled."

Such perfect correspondence should not be ignored or denied by Bible students. While we may ponder whether the "time, times and half a time" is a literal 42 months, the one thing that is indisputable is that the critical eschatological time reference has to do with the fate of Israel and the city of Jerusalem. What is also indisputable is that this time reference would be fulfilled, "when the power of the holy people has been completely shattered." And this is undeniably the fall of Jerusalem in AD 70.

The correspondence of all of this to the time when all prophecy would be fully accomplished should be more than apparent.

Daniel 9 deals with the seventy weeks and by the end of that divine period, vision and prophecy would be finished– fully accomplished. Daniel 12 foretold the time of the end, the resurrection, which is, as we have seen, when all prophecy would be fulfilled.

Likewise, Revelation 10-11 foretold the time when Daniel 12 would be fully accomplished, the time when "the mystery of God" declared by the prophets" would be finished. And this would be, just as in Daniel 9 and in Daniel 12, the time of the judgment on the "holy people and the holy city."

I must add here a few additional thoughts on Revelation 11 and its impact on the postmillennial world.

It is, as we have noted, admitted by virtually all futurists that the resurrection is the time of the fulfillment of all prophecy. With that in mind, take a look at the comparative chart between Revelation 11 and Revelation 20.

Revelation 11:15-19	Revelation 20-21
Promise of the resurrection	Promise of the resurrection
The hope of Israel	The hope of Israel
When all prophecy fulfilled (Revelation 10:6-7)[201]	When all prophecy fulfilled
Resurrection at the seventh trump– The last trump	Resurrection at the "last trump" - (1 Corinthians 15:52)
Rewarding of those in the books (Daniel 12:1-2)	Rewarding of those in the books (Revelation 20:12)
Rewarding of the dead- the prophets- eternal life– the kingdom	Rewarding of the dead- the prophets- eternal life– the kingdom
Vindication of the martyrs	Vindication of the martyrs, i.e. "the rest of the dead" that come to life at the end of the millennium are the full number of the martyrs of Revelation 6:11.
Postmillennialists commonly apply Revelation 10-11 to the end of the Old Covenant Age in AD 70.	The question is: What is the hermeneutic of distinction between Revelation 10-11 and Revelation 20-22?

---

[201] We need to be reminded that Jesus said the events surrounding the end of Israel's age was when "all things that are written must be fulfilled" (Luke 21:22).

Many of the leading postmillennialists of the day insist that Revelation 10-11 were fulfilled in the AD 70 judgment of Old Covenant Jerusalem.[202] This really is significant.

The question has to be asked, what is the distinction between Revelation 10-11 and Revelation 20f. It is surely arbitrary and capricious to simply say that Revelation 10-11 was fulfilled in AD 70, but that Revelation 20f remains to be fulfilled at the end of the Christian age.

How can one maintain that the resurrection of Revelation 11 was in AD 70– which would fulfill all things that are written– and then turn around and claim that Revelation 20 is about the fulfillment of all prophecy? *You cannot fulfill all things over and over and over again.* The fulfillment of all things is, well, the fulfillment of all things.

So, just as Jesus said that in the fall of Jerusalem, "these be the days of vengeance when all things that are written must be fulfilled" Daniel and Revelation agree in positing the time of total fulfillment as the time of the judgment of Old Covenant Jerusalem.

Each of the verses noted above agree in positing the eschatological consummation, and the fulfillment of all prophecy, at the end of Israel's covenant age. Thus, Jesus' words that not one iota of Torah would pass until it was all fulfilled points inexorably to that time, that framework, that consummation.

The fact is that Jesus and even the OT posited the fulfillment of all things– the consummation of the process of fulfilment *initiated by John* the Baptizer (Matthew 17. 10-12; Luke 16:16) at the end of the Old Covenant age in AD 70. I believe Scott McKnight is correct– although he did not develop or discuss the full implications of his comments:

"I will argue that Jesus saw no further than A.D. 70 and that he thought everything would be wrapped up in conjunction with that catastrophic event for Israel. In seeing the future this way, Jesus

---

[202] This is the view of DeMar, (*Madness*, 1994, p. 173, 264, 288, 290, etc.); McDurmon, *Jesus V Jerusalem*, 114); Mathison, *Postmillennialism*, 151+); Jordan, (Garden, tape 6). Gentry, (2009, 408) likewise says that the sounding of the seventh trump "declares that Israel's time is up."

was not mistaken; rather, he envisioned the future very much like the Jewish prophets of the Israelite tradition did and not all that different from the way of contemporary Jewish prophets."[203] He continues: "Jesus prophesied of the destruction of Jerusalem as the climactic event in Israel's history that would end the privilege of Israel in God's plan. He also attached to this the final resolution of Israel through the images connected with remnant and redemption." (1999, p. 138).

McKnight says that the church continued to look for the eschatological consummation beyond AD 70, however. And in this is found one of the greatest of all theological tragedies. The Great Apostasy stripped the church of its roots and the church looked for a materialistic, literalistic end of the age at the end of time, instead of seeing the spiritual import of what had admittedly happened.

[203] Scott McKnight, *A New Vision for Israel*, (Eerdmans, Grand Rapids, 1999)139.

THESE BE THE DAYS OF VENGEANCE IN WHICH ALL THINGS THAT ARE WRITTEN MUST BE FULFILLED
When Was All Fulfilled?
Luke 21:22
A Response to Kenneth Gentry

Kenneth Gentry is a scholar for whom I have a great deal of respect. I appreciate his exegetical skills, normally. However, Gentry is an outspoken critic of Covenant Eschatology and occasionally writes against it, although he has adamantly refused to engage me in formal debate, either written or public.

Dr. Gentry clearly thinks that he has found a fatal flaw in the preterist argument on Luke 21:22. I want to respond to his article, and demonstrate that it is not the true preterist eschatology that is flawed, but the futurist. The erudite Dr. Gentry is really excellent in his critiques of dispensationalism. However, when it comes to Covenant Eschatology, his logically is fatally flawed.

Here are Gentry's main arguments from his blog and review of his revised book *He Shall Have Dominion*.[204]

<< In its context Luke 21:22 reads as follows: "But when you see Jerusalem surrounded by armies, then recognize that her desolation is at hand. Then let those who are in Judea flee to the mountains, and let those who are in the midst of the city depart, and let not those who are in the country enter the city; because these are days of vengeance, in order that all things which are written may be fulfilled" (Lk 21:20-22).

Unarguably, (sic) the context here is focusing on AD 70, as even dispensationalists agree.

The hyper-preterists naively assume that Jesus is speaking globally of absolutely all prophecies when he declares that "all things which are written" will be fulfilled in AD 70. They hold, therefore, that no prophecy remains, which means that prophecies regarding the resurrection of all men, the second coming, and more came to pass in AD 70. They base their argument on deficient hermeneutics. Note just

---

[204] Gentry's book is advertised at (https://www.kennethgentry.com/catalog/product_info.php?products_id=432).

one deadly observation against their approach: The grammar of the passage limits the declaration. Jesus speaks of "all things which are written," by employing a perfect passive participle: /gegrammena/("having been written"). This refers to prophecies already written — when he speaks in AD 30. Yet we know that more prophecies arise later in the New Testament revelation.

Once again we see a limitation on Jesus' statement. Furthermore, technically it does not even refer to any prophecy which Christ speaks. For these are not prophecies that have already been written. That being the case, the final resurrection (for instance) is outside of this declaration (Jn 5:28-29).

Thus, Jesus is referring to all things written in the Old Testament. At this stage of redemptive history those are the only prophecies that had already been written. (end quote, DKP)

Quite frankly, *I could hardly believe what I was reading* from the pen of the erudite Dr. Gentry. He has engaged in numerous debates, and surely knows that one must be careful in making polemic arguments. The absolute desperation, the *total failure of logic* on the part of Dr. Gentry is glaring and egregious.

Let me summarize Dr. Gentry's argument for ease of understanding.

When Jesus said (Luke 21:22), that, "all things written must be fulfilled," he referred only to those prophecies (and *all* of those prophecies), that had been written prior to his statement in AD 30.

All New Testament prophecies of the resurrection (e.g. John 5:28f, 1 Corinthians 15, 1 Thessalonians, etc.), were written after AD 30.

Therefore, all New Testament prophecies of the resurrection were not part of the "all things that are written" that were to be fulfilled in the fall of Jerusalem in AD 70.

Here is what Dr. Gentry concludes: "Thus, Jesus is referring to all things written in the Old Testament. At this stage of redemptive history

171

those are the only prophecies that had already been written."

Gentry's "logic" fails on a number of points. But, I will only make two points in response to his article.

Argument #1– The New Testament prophecies of the resurrection are simply the reiteration of the Old Testament prophecies *(things already "having been written" in AD 30).*

Proof of this argument: I need only refer to the words of Paul. The apostle affirmed in the most unambiguous manner that his doctrine of the resurrection was *nothing* but that found in the Old Testament, i.e. *in that which had already been written*!

Acts 24:14-15: "But this I confess to you, that according to the Way which they call a sect, so I worship the God of my fathers, believing all things which are written in the Law and in the Prophets. I have hope in God, which they themselves also accept, that there will be a resurrection of the dead, both of the just and the unjust."

Paul said his doctrine of the resurrection of the dead, for which he was on trial, was found in Moses and the Law and the prophets. That certainly qualifies as that which was written before AD 30.

Acts 26:21-23– "Having therefore obtained help of God, I continue unto this day, witnessing both to small and great, saying none other things than those which the prophets and Moses did say should come: That Christ should suffer, and that he should be the first that should rise from the dead, and should shew light unto the people, and to the Gentiles."

Paul said he preached nothing, *nothing* but the hope of Israel found in Moses and the prophets.

Paul taught of the resurrection of the dead.

Therefore, the doctrine of the resurrection of the dead was found in Moses and the prophets.

In stark contrast to what Paul said, remember Boettner's claim that it is the NT exclusively that provides information for "Christian eschatology."

There could hardly be a more explicit contrast between the two "gospels." Paul's eschatology was nothing but the hope of Israel found in the OT; Boettner (and many postmillennialists to varying degrees), say that the OT holds nothing for us in regards to eschatology. Boettner is at odds with scripture.

Romans 8:23– 9:1-4-- "And not only they, but ourselves also, which have the first fruits of the Spirit, even we ourselves groan within ourselves, waiting for the *adoption*, to wit, the redemption of our body... For I could wish that myself were accursed from Christ for my brethren, my kinsmen according to the flesh: 4 Who are Israelites; *to whom pertaineth the adoption*, and the glory, and the covenants, and the giving of the law, and the service of God, and the promises."

The adoption, according to Paul, was the resurrection.
But, the promise of the adoption was given to, and belonged to, Israel after the flesh.
This means that the adoption, the promise of the resurrection, was from the Old Testament promises made to Israel after the flesh.

I need to note here that there is a "new" form of eschatology manifesting itself these days. Actually, it is not truly new, but, it is devised with the specific intent to refute Covenant Eschatology.

The claim is made that God did fulfill His promises to Israel in AD 70, but, that the "real" promises of the New Creation, the restoration of all things, belongs to the new Israel of God, the church, to bring to fruition at the end of time. This is simply a modified form of "Replacement theology." It overlooks or denies that the eschatological resurrection, "the redemption of the body" was the promise given to Israel "after the flesh" (Romans 8:23- 9:3). It was that end of the millennium hope, "to which our twelve tribes, earnestly serving God night and day, hope to attain" (Acts 26:7).

173

Paul knew nothing of an imminent, preliminary resurrection for Israel of the flesh, i.e. in fulfillment of Daniel 12,[205] and then, another, consummative resurrection, promised to Israel of the Spirit.

This doctrine turns God's method of operation 180% out. God has always operated from *the natural to the spiritual*. But, in this new theology– as in much of futurism– this is reversed. Israel received her *spiritual resurrection*, but, the *physical resurrection* is still future. This is a theological invention, that denies Paul's repeated comments that his one eschatological hope was the hope of Israel.

Finally, of course, this "new" theology completely ignores the fact that Peter, anticipating the "restoration of all things, foretold by all the prophets" said that: "all the prophets, from Samuel and those who follow, as many as have spoken, have also foretold these days" (Acts 3:24).

In the new paradigm, however, Peter was clearly wrong. All of the prophets did not speak of his day as the time for the restoration of all things, they spoke of times far, far removed from his days; so far, two millennia removed.

1 Corinthians 15:54-55-- "So when this corruptible shall have put on incorruption, and this mortal shall have put on immortality, then shall be brought to pass the saying that is written, Death is swallowed up in victory. O death, where is thy sting? O grave, where is thy victory?" Paul cites Isaiah 25:8 and Hosea 13:14 as the source of his resurrection doctrine in Corinthians.

---

[205] We have noted above the stunning changes in the postmillennial world in regard to Daniel 12. The orthodox reformed view of Daniel has always been that Daniel 12:2 predicted the end of the millennium resurrection. This was Calvin's view, and that of the creeds. Yet now, as we have seen, modern reformers are openly rejecting the historical, orthodox, reformed view of Daniel, and saying that Daniel actually foretold the spiritual resurrection of the corporate body of Israel in AD 70. Further, we are being told that we should not be overly concerned that Calvin and the creeds missed the point of Daniel! This is an incredible development that is not receiving enough attention.

174

Paul said that the resurrection would be when Isaiah 25 and Hosea 13:14 would be fulfilled.[206]

Thus, the resurrection hope and doctrine of 1 Corinthians 15 was found in, and based on the Old Testament prophecies made to Israel. From these texts, it is undeniable that the resurrection hope expressed by the New Testament writers was nothing other than a reiteration of what had already been written long ago in the Old Testament scriptures. This is *fatal* to Gentry's argument and theology. Indisputably, the New Testament prophecies of the resurrection are grounded in and based on the Old Covenant prophecies. To say otherwise is to deny Paul who said he preached nothing but the hope of Israel found in Moses and the prophets. 1 Corinthians 15 is not different from Isaiah 25 or Hosea 13:14. Paul says that when the resurrection occurred, it would be the fulfillment of those prophecies. To say that 1 Corinthians 15 is the explication of those prophecies is not the same as saying that they are different from those prophecies.

You cannot say that all Old Testament prophecies were fulfilled at the AD 70 parousia of Christ therefore, without affirming the fulfillment of all New Testament eschatology. There is no "new" eschatology in the New Testament. *All New Testament eschatology is the anticipation of the imminent fulfillment of Old Testament promises.* Period. This totally falsifies Gentry's specious argument.[207]

---

[206] In a stunningly desperate argument, Jerry McDonald, in our written debate, argued that Isaiah 25 did not actually predict the resurrection! I must admit that I was shocked at his claim. So, per McDonald's "logic" even though Paul said his doctrine of the resurrection was from the OT, and even though he said that when the mortal would put on immortality, that "then shall be brought to pass the saying" and he then quotes directly from Isaiah (and Hosea) that *in reality*, Isaiah had nothing to do with what Paul was predicting! Such illogical, desperate "arguments" reveal the indefensible nature of the amillennial paradigm. That debate can be found on my websites: www.eschatology.org, and www.bibleprophecy.com.

[207] In numerous formal debates with both amillennialists and postmillennialists, this has been the critical point of controversy. Amillennialists particularly are at a total loss to deal with this indisputable Biblical fact. Even James

What is astounding to consider in light of Gentry's argument above is that *Gentry believes that the Old Testament did indeed predict the resurrection of the dead at the end of the Christian age!*

In his book, *The Greatness of the Great Commission*,[208] Gentry cited Daniel 12:2 as predictive of the resurrection "at the end of history." Note: We would be remiss if we did not take note of Gentry's recent, radical change in his application of Daniel 12.Without noting his remarkable change, Gentry now – *with true preterists*– sees Daniel 12 as fulfilled at the end of the Old Covenant age in AD 70 (*Dominion*, 2009, 538).

So, consider what this does for Dr. Gentry:

All Old Testament prophecy would be fulfilled by the time of, and in the events of the fall of Jerusalem in AD 70. (Kenneth Gentry)

But, the Old Testament predicted the general resurrection of the dead (Daniel 12:2, Kenneth Gentry).

Therefore, the general resurrection of the dead occurred in the events of the fall of Jerusalem in AD 70.

Yet, Gentry now applies Daniel 12 to AD 70. This is, needless to say, a *radical* change from his earlier view, and yet he has given no

---

Jordan, postmillennialist, admitted that all of God's OT promises to Israel were fulfilled no later than AD 70, but then attempted to posit a yet future eschaton. My debate with Jordan is now available in book form, from my websites, Amazon, and other retailers. As we have documented above, other postmillennialists affirm the complete fulfillment and removal of Torah no later than AD 70. Gentry is not, therefore, positing an idiosyncratic view of the fulfillment of OT prophecy in AD 70.

[208] (Tyler, Tx., Institute for Christian Economics, 1993)142.

indication of that change.[209] This likewise puts him at odds with the huge majority of scholarship, church history and the creeds. One can but wonder if the on-going controversy with what Gentry disparagingly calls "hyper-preterism" has spawned Gentry's "conversion." He now takes the preterist view of Daniel 12, while condemning preterists for their views.

We have established point #1 beyond any possibility of refutation. This point alone totally destroys Gentry's attempt at refuting Covenant Eschatology.

Argument #2– For argument sake therefore, I will gladly accept Dr. Gentry's summary statement: "Thus, Jesus is referring to *all things written in the Old Testament.* At this stage of redemptive history those are the only prophecies that had already been written." (My emphasis, DKP).

Once again, Gentry has falsified his own eschatology. Consider the following argument:

All things written in the Old Testament, i.e. all Old Testament prophecy, was fulfilled by the time of, and in the events of, the fall of Jerusalem in AD 70. (Kenneth Gentry).

But, the Old Testament prophesied of the resurrection of the dead (Acts 24:14f; 26:6f; 26:21f, Romans 8:23-9:1-4, 1 Corinthians 15:55-56).

---

[209] Interestingly, in his revised *Dominion*, (2009, 495, n. 45) Gentry takes note that dispensationalist Dwight Pentecost had radically altered his views over the years yet had not acknowledged or indicated that change in his later writings. He says Pentecost's "radical shift" in his application of some key eschatological texts, "does not seem to him to compromise his eschatological system." Yet, Gentry has made an astoundingly radical shift in his application of one of the key eschatological texts, and yet has not indicated that change in his writings so far as we can determine. He has *done* what he chides Pentecost for doing!

177

Therefore, the prophecies of the resurrection of the dead were fulfilled by the time of, and in the events of, the fall of Jerusalem in AD 70.

This argument is *prima facie* true. (Let me take note again that there is a growing movement within the postmillennial world positing the fulfillment of Daniel 12:2 at AD 70. This is now Gentry's view, DeMar, McDurmon, and others. To say that this is a stunning development– and a radical departure from traditional postmillennialism is to greatly understate the case).

It is *incontrovertibly true* that the Old Testament foretold the resurrection of the dead. Kenneth Gentry agrees– even if he no longer applies Daniel 12 to that event

It is *irrefutably true* that all New Testament prophecies of the resurrection are drawn from and the reiteration of the Old Testament prophecies.

It is *undeniable* that Jesus said that all things written would be fulfilled by the time of, and in the events of the fall of Jerusalem in AD 70.

Gentry is correct in affirming that *all Old Testament prophecies* would be fulfilled at / in AD 70. And this proves, *beyond refutation*, that the resurrection of the dead came at the dissolution of the Old Covenant age of Israel in AD 70.

Incidentally, it would do no good for Mr. Gentry, or anyone else, to amend his statement and argue that all that Jesus really meant was that all Old Covenant prophecies *concerning the fall of Jerusalem* were to be fulfilled in AD 70. (You will note that Gentry made no attempt to limit the scope of the Old Covenant prophecies to be fulfilled in AD 70. He said emphatically, "Jesus is referring to *all things written in the Old Testament*"). Likewise, when DeMar stated that as a non-dispensationalist he believes:"All promises made to Israel have been fulfilled", he did not qualify the "all." Neither did Mathison when he said, "Christians are now experiencing the fulfillment of the eschatological hopes of Israel."

The fact is that these men are on record as believing that all OT prophecy has been fulfilled, and that God was through with Israel (more specifically, Judah) in AD 70.

The indisputable fact is that in the Old Testament the resurrection of the dead is *repeatedly* posited at the destruction of Old Covenant Israel. Note a couple of examples.

* Isaiah 25:1-8–

"O LORD, You are my God. I will exalt You, I will praise Your name, For You have done wonderful things; Your counsels of old are faithfulness and truth. 2 For You have made a city a ruin, A fortified city a ruin, A palace of foreigners to be a city no more; It will never be rebuilt. 3 Therefore the strong people will glorify You; The city of the terrible nations will fear You. 4 For You have been a strength to the poor, A strength to the needy in his distress, A refuge from the storm, A shade from the heat; For the blast of the terrible ones is as a storm against the wall. 5 You will reduce the noise of aliens, As heat in a dry place; As heat in the shadow of a cloud, The song of the terrible ones will be diminished. 6 And in this mountain The LORD of hosts will make for all people A feast of choice pieces, A feast of wines on the lees, Of fat things full of marrow, Of well–refined wines on the lees. 7 And He will destroy on this mountain The surface of the covering cast over all people, And the veil that is spread over all nations. 8 He will swallow up death forever, And the Lord GOD will wipe away tears from all faces; The rebuke of His people He will take away from all the earth; For the LORD has spoken."

Note that in the day that YHVH would destroy death, it would also be when He made the city a desolation and turned the temple over to foreigners. The city under consideration is the "city of confusion" in

179

chapter 24:10f, Ariel, i.e. Jerusalem.[210] So, Isaiah emphatically posits the resurrection at the time of Jerusalem's demise.

* In chapter 26:19-21, the Lord predicted the resurrection at the time when YHVH would come out of heaven and avenge the blood of the martyrs. Of course, Jesus was emphatically clear that all of the righteous blood of all the saints, shed on the earth, would be avenged in the judgment of Jerusalem in AD 70 (Matthew 23:34f).

* In Isaiah 27:1f, we find the destruction of Leviathan, the enemy of God, defeated in the day that the Lord would come, the Day of 26:19f, i.e. the day of the resurrection. And, this Day of the Lord would also be when the people that YHVH had created would no longer receive mercy, and He would turn the altar to chalkstones (Isaiah 27:9f). Thus, again, the resurrection is clearly placed in the context of the judgment of Jerusalem and Israel.

Likewise, the very passage that Gentry once appealed to for the resurrection at the end of the age, Daniel 12:2, says that the resurrection would be, "when the power of the holy people is completely shattered" (Daniel 12:2-7). And of course, Gentry and other postmillennialists, as we have seen, now agrees with this. See my book, *Seventy Weeks Are Determined...For the Resurrection*, for a full discussion of this passage. There are in fact several OT passages that posit the resurrection in the context of the judgment of Israel.

The point of course is that it will do Gentry no good whatsoever to now say that all that Jesus really meant to say was, "these be the days of vengeance in which all things that are written about the fall of Jerusalem will be fulfilled." On one level, we could agree with this, for

---

[210] Significantly, McDurmon, (2011, 59) commenting on Isaiah 24 took note of the fact that the destruction of the creation, the establishment of the kingdom, etc. found in Isaiah 24 must be seen within the context of God's judgment of Israel, because the destruction comes as a direct result of Israel's violation of Torah. McDurmon conveniently overlooks the fact, however, that the Messianic Banquet and the resurrection are inextricably bound up with that sequence of events and the covenantal context.

as demonstrated, the fall of Jerusalem was in fact to be the time of the resurrection!

So, Gentry boasts that the "hyper-preterists" make a "naive" claim about Luke 21:22. He says we are guilty of "deficient hermeneutics." He claims to have made a "deadly observation" against the preterist argument.

In fact, Gentry has exposed his own desperation and his own naive and deficient hermeneutic. We have made what is in fact "a deadly observation" in response to Gentry's specious argument.

Kenneth Gentry has, *through his own argument*, destroyed his postmillennial, futurist eschatology. He has actually confirmed the truthfulness of "hyper-preterism!"

By arguing that the fall of Jerusalem in AD 70 was the time of the fulfillment of "all Old Testament prophecy" Gentry– and other postmillennialists– have inadvertently falsified their own futurist eschatology. The Old Testament prophecies included the "Second Coming" of Christ, the judgment at the end of the age, and the resurrection!

SUMMARY

Jesus's words in Matthew 5:17-18 are difficult to escape. And yet, they are so challenging to modern evangelical Christianity's view of the passing of Torah, that a host of sometimes widely speculative "arguments" are offered in order to escape the force of those words: "Not one jot or one tittle shall pass from the law, until it is all fulfilled."

What we have done in this volume #1 is to demonstrate from both the Old Covenant and the New that there is a united testimony concerning when all prophecy, when all of the law, was to be fully accomplished. That time of fulfillment was not to be the end of time or the end of human history. It was to be at the full end of the Old Covenant age of Israel in the fall of Jerusalem, which occurred in AD 70.

While various attempts are made to escape the force and meaning of Jesus' words in Matthew 5, we have shown that these attempts are futile. Virtually all of the objections noted either explicitly or implicitly distort and deny Jesus' words.

Both amillennialists and postmillennialists insist that the law of Moses died, either at the cross or in AD 70. Both paradigms say that God's covenant with Israel was fulfilled, and that ethnic Israel's promises no longer serve as YHVH's covenant. Yet, the Sabbath and the feast days of Torah, as well as circumcision, were intrinsic elements of God's covenant with Israel, and pointed directly to the eschatological consummation of the resurrection. To argue therefore, that Torah and Israel have been fulfilled and are now passe, is to tacitly affirm the fulfillment of Israel's eschatological promises– including the resurrection of the dead. This is a glaring and major inconsistency in these paradigms.

While the dispensationalists see Israel as the centerpiece of God's eschatological schema, they overlook and deny the timing and nature of the fulfillment, and they, like the postmillennialist and amillennialists, say that the Law of Moses has passed away.

So, while all futurist eschatologies claim that the Law of Moses was removed in the first century, they then insist that the prophecies embedded in God's covenant with Israel, firmly and intrinsically a part of the typological, sacrificial, cultic world, have not yet been fulfilled. As we have stated repeatedly, this is a logical fallacy of major proportions.

We have not only examined the attempts to mitigate Jesus' words, but we have demonstrated from scripture that Biblically, "the law" was a comprehensive term, encompassing the entirety of what we commonly call the Old Testament. There are no contextual qualifiers in Matthew 5 that allows us to escape the comprehensive definition therefore of "the law."

That means that until all the law was fulfilled, none of it would pass.

It means that until the Psalms, which were "the law" was fulfilled, none of Torah would pass.

It means that until all prophecy, which was "the law" was fully accomplished, not one jot or one tittle of the Tanakh would pass.

It means that until what the typological Sabbaths, the New Moons and feast days, all of which were "the law," was fully realized that not one of these things ceased to be binding and valid as "shadows of good things about to come."

Jesus' words resound down to the present moment, and without major linguistic, textual and contextual gymnastics, are unavoidable: "Not one jot or one tittle shall pass from the law until it is all fulfilled." And according to numerous Biblical passages in both the Old Covenant and the New, the time for the fulfillment of all of "the law" was at the end of the Old Covenant age of Israel in AD 70. The fulfillment of all things written does not await the end of time, or the end of the Christian age.

In the volumes to follow, we will establish this even more.

Scripture Index

(Written and Compiled by Samuel G. Dawson)

Topic Index

(Written and Compiled by Samuel G. Dawson)

Feast of Harvest represented the
resurrection 66
Feast of Trumpets represented
the judgment 66
feast of unleavened bread, no one
denies pointed to resurrection
115
feast of weeks, pointed to resurrection and establishment of the
church 115
foreshadowed eschatological
events 54
if not fulfilled then entirety of Torah remains 66
intrinscially prophetic 115
passover, no one denies pointed
to Jesus 115
Pentecost, pointed to resurrection
and the establishment of the
church 115
predictive 115
sabbath represented salvation 66
were called the law 136
Filson, Floyd, on messianic banquet
32
Filson, Floyd *The Gospel According to Matthew* 32
Four Views of the Millennium, Lorraine Boettner 48
France, R. T.
eschatology of OT wasn't concerned with the end of the
world 17
Jews had no doctrine or concept
of end of time 16
on messianic banquet 32
France, R. T. *Jesus and the Old Testament* 17
Frost, Sam *Exegetical Essays on the
Resurrection of the Dead* 52
fulfilled, when were all things? 151-
169
futurists divorce Heb. 11-12 from
Rev. 20-22 37

G

gathering
of the people in Isa. 11 taking
place in Paul's ministry falsifies postponement of Israel's
kingdom 28
of the people of the Lord
Isa. 11.10 28
Rom. 15.12f 28
Gentry, Kenneth
a response to 170-
applies Dan. 12 to AD 70 176
believes OT predicted resurrection at the end of the Christian
age 176
chastises Dwight Pentecost for
radical changes while he does
the same 177
confirms the truthfulness of hyper-preterism 181
ignores Mt.5.17-18 123
Mosaic Law eternal 2
openly rejects the foundational eschatology of the creeds 95
Gentry, Kenneth *He Shall Have Dominion*, a response to 170-
Gentry, Kenneth *House Divided,
The Break-up of Dispensational
Theology* 2
Gentry, Kenneth *The Greatness of
the Great Commission* 176
Gentry, Kenneth *Thine is the Kingdom* 96
Goppelt, Leonard *The Typological
Interpretation of the Old Testament* 65
gospel
a spiritual law to govern a spiri-
tual people 107
didn't replace Mosaic Law as a
nationalistic constitution 107
Gray,Timothy *The Temple In The
Gospel of Mark* 102
Great and Terrible Day of the Lord
Chaldean invasion called in
Zeph. 1-2 110

Z

Made in the USA
San Bernardino, CA
04 January 2018